H. Martens, del.t

Day & Haghe, Lith.rs to the Queen

HEROIC CONDUCT of FOUR PRIVATES of H.M. 31st REG.t at the BATTLE of MAZEENA.

# NARRATIVE
## OF THE
## LATE VICTORIOUS CAMPAIGN
### IN
# AFGHANISTAN
## UNDER GENERAL POLLOCK

WITH RECOLLECTIONS OF
SEVEN YEARS' SERVICE IN INDIA

LIEUTENANT GREENWOOD
H.M. 31st REGIMENT

**The Naval & Military Press Ltd**

published in association with

**FIREPOWER
The Royal Artillery Museum**
Woolwich

Published by
**The Naval & Military Press Ltd**
Unit 10 Ridgewood Industrial Park,
Uckfield, East Sussex,
TN22 5QE England
Tel: +44 (0) 1825 749494
Fax: +44 (0) 1825 765701
www.naval-military-press.com

*in association with*

**FIREPOWER**
**The Royal Artillery Museum, Woolwich**
www.firepower.org.uk

*In reprinting in facsimile from the original, any imperfections are inevitably reproduced and the quality may fall short of modern type and cartographic standards.*

Printed and bound by Antony Rowe Ltd, Eastbourne

TO

## MAJOR GENERAL SIR COLIN HALKETT,

KNIGHT COMMANDER OF THE BATH,

GRAND CROSS OF THE GUELPHIC ORDER,

COLONEL OF THE 31st REGIMENT.

&c. &c. &c.

---

Sir,

I feel very great satisfaction in availing myself of the permission which you have given me to dedicate to you the accompanying Narrative. The urbanity and consideration which have invariably marked your conduct towards those under your command, claim at their hands the best tribute of respect which they may be able to render.

With the highest regard,

I have the honour to remain, Sir,

Your most obliged and humble servant,

The Author.

## ADVERTISEMENT.

It may be necessary for the Author to state that the present volume was commenced from a simple desire of laying before his countrymen such details relative to the late victorious Campaign in Affghanistan, as occurred under his own immediate observation and experience. He ventures to hope that the plain unvarnished narrative of the strange circumstances, and of the hardships and dangers encountered and surmounted by our gallant soldiers in the far East, will not prove unacceptable to the numerous readers who must feel interested in their perilous adventures and exploits, which so materially conduced to determine the extent of the British rule in India at the present moment.

The writer has, moreover, endeavoured to record his impressions of the wonders that every where greeted him on his arrival in the East, the plains and jungles of which attracted his ardour as a sportsman; and he trusts that the few precepts and lessons which he has introduced for the benefit of his younger "brothers in arms," as well as for those who are about to embrace the profession, may not be altogether without their value.

J. GREENWOOD.

Cumberland Terrace,
  Regent's Park,
    March 1844.

# CONTENTS.

## CHAPTER I.

Page

Original destination—Early visions of greatness—Hanover and its Military Academy—A commission obtained, and its first effects on the mind—The depôt and its occupations—Preparations for India, and advice to young officers . . . . . 1

## CHAPTER II.

Author embarks for India—Shipmasters on shore different persons from shipmasters at sea—Reflections on leaving home—Story of a shark—The flying Dutchman—Catching turtle in a calm—First sight of India—Pilot comes on board—Anecdote of a tiger—Shooting at Diamond Harbour—Arrival at Calcutta—Indian servants—Indian cities—The beggars—Fakirs—Marriage processions—Hospitality of the European residents of Calcutta . . . . 18

## CHAPTER III.

March up the country—Shooting on the road—Sight of a tiger—Killing a bear—A shot at a fakir—Making bear's grease—A sirloin of bear's flesh—Pariah dogs—Jungle fever—H.M. 49th Regiment—Dâk travelling—Arrival at Dinapore . . . 42

## CHAPTER IV.

Page

Sporting at Dinapore—Snipe shooting—Tiger hunting—Indigo planters at Tirhoot—Anecdote of a lion—A Tiger hunter in an unpleasant situation—Jungle fowl—Runaway elephants—Jungle bees—Catching wild elephants—Sagacity of elephants—Hog hunting—A pig-sticking griff—Bobbery pack—Treatment of dogs and horses—Syces and grass-cutters — Horse-dealers — Races — Sailing on the Ganges—Anecdotes—Sporting griffs, &c. . . 63

## CHAPTER V.

Departure from Dinapore—Station of Ghazeepore—Attah of roses—Duck-shooting—Indian thieves—Showers of fish—Fruits—The pine-apple—Snakes, musk-rats and mosquitoes—Agra—The Taj Mahal—Ruins—Wolves—Famine at Agra—Sporting at Agra—Grand entertainment given by the Rajah of Bhurtpore—Ice establishment . . . . . 98

## CHAPTER VI.

Rumours of war—Departure from Agra—Arrival at Meerut—March towards Affghanistan—Women of the 44th—The Begum Sumroo—Manufacture of shawls at Loodianah—Camels—Cross the Sutledge—The Punjab—Loss of baggage—The irregular horse—Forced marches—The Seiks—Crossing rivers—Cheyt Sing—Burial of the dead, &c. . . . 123

## CHAPTER VII.

Arrival at Peshawur—General Avitabili—Entertainments—Nautch girls—Hurree Singh—The Kyber pass—Ali Musjid—Scarcity of water—Heroism of a Sepoy—Brigadier Monteath—Skirmish with Kyberees—Jellalabad . . . . . . . 151

## CHAPTER VIII.

March to Pesh Bolak—Destruction of forts—Death of two officers—Their graves outraged—The Shinwarrees—Battle of Mazeena—Heroic conduct of four soldiers of H.M. 31st Regiment—Return to Jellalabad—Sickness in camp—March towards Cabul—Remains of the 44th—Forcing the Jugdulluck pass—Dead bodies in the pass—Narrow escapes—Kuttasung—A take in for the Affghans—A forced march—Arrival at Tezeen . . . . . . . 178

## CHAPTER IX.

Valley of Tezeen—Night attack—Battle of Tezeen—Storming the left heights—A charge of bayonets—A fat chief—Arrival at Koord Cabul—Scene within the pass—Arrival at Cabul—Rescue of the prisoners—Noble conduct of Akbar Khan—Capture of Cabul—British Flag hoisted in the Bala Hissar—Artillery taken—Extraordinary recovery of a Will—Arrival of General Nott—Battle of Istaliff—Destruction of Cabul . . . . . . . . 209

## CHAPTER X.

General Elphinstone's retreat—Errors committed—Dr. Brydon—His perilous escape—General Pollock issues orders to retrograde—Difficulties of the march—The Koord Cabul pass—Conveyance of an Affghan trophy—Narrow escape of a courier—Jugdulluck—Engagement with the Affghans—Luxurious repast—Gundamuck—Futtiabad—Jellalabad . . 246

## CHAPTER XI.

Destruction of Jellalabad—Passage of the Choota Kyber—The Kyber pass—A forced march—Peshawur—The Punjab—Mortality among the soldiers—The triumphal arch—Arrival at Ferozepore—A dâk trip—A storm—Difficulties by the way—Drunken Seiks—Arrival at Meerut . . . . . . . 277

## CHAPTER XII.

Station of Meerut—Dâk trip to Calcutta—Station of Allahabad—Benares—Beggars—The Rajmahal hills—A Tiger—A wild elephant—Arrival at Calcutta—Author embarks for England—Fishing off the coast of Africa—Table Bay—Cape Town—St. Helena—A gale of wind—An Irish hooker—Kinsale—An Irish steamer—An accident—Arrival at home . . 311

## CHAPTER XIII.—SUPPLEMENTARY.

Remarks on India—The Indian Army—Native Regiments—Singular feat—Lieutenant Mayne—Horse artillery—Captain Abbot's troop—Foot artillery—Costume and pay—Penurious system—The sepoys—Local corps—Officer's pensions—Pay of officers—A subaltern's expenses—" Boat allowance"—Troops in the Presidencies—Anglo-Indian army—The Seiks—The Zemindars—Affairs of the Punjab—Hopes for the future . . . . . . . . 338

# ILLUSTRATIONS.

Heroic conduct of Four Privates of H.M. 31st
    Regiment at the Battle of Mazeena . *Frontispiece*.
Fort of Jumrood, in the Plain of Peshawur . . 154
Fort of Allee Musjid, in the Kyber Pass . . 157
City and Valley of Cabul . . . . . 237
Bala Hissar, or Citadel, at Cabul . . . 235
Map of Affghanistan, and of the Route pursued
    by the British Army to Cabul. . *End of the volume.*

# NARRATIVE,

&c.

---

## CHAPTER I.

Original destination—Early visions of greatness—Hanover and its Military Academy—A commission obtained, and its first effects on the mind—The depôt and its occupations—Preparations for India, and advice to young officers.

GREAT individuals are often ushered into the world by strange events. None of these portentous signs, I believe, occurred at my nativity. I entered upon this busy universe of ours in a very common-place manner, without shewing any particular signs of one day being likely to set the Thames on fire, or of performing any equally extraordinary feat.

My dear mother intended me for the Church, in which, of course, I was to be a shining light; in fact, nothing but the Archbishopric of Canterbury seemed to her fond imagination to be the goal which I was destined to attain. Reading I delighted in as a child; but the lives of Lord Nelson, our illustrious Duke, and Napoleon Buonaparte were the themes on which I doated; and while my kind parents delighted their fond hearts with the idea of what a scholar their dear studious boy would one day be, I was treasuring up in my young mind the accounts of all my heroes' battles, and hugging the thought, foolish child as I was, that one day my achievements might rival theirs, and England ring again with the story of my victories. That was the age of romance, and it passed away; but when I arrived at maturer years, I still determined to be nothing but a soldier. Then, however, instead of leading armies and ruling the destinies of empires, the command of a regiment was the summit of my hopes.

My kind parents, although disappointed in their anticipations of my becoming a learned prelate, lent their best endeavours to forward my views in the only profession that I would hear of. But a commission was not quite to be had for the asking; and on application they heard that some months, perhaps years, must elapse before I had any chance of obtaining a legitimate right to be shot at for five and threepence a-day, which, be it known to my non-militant readers, is the pay of an ensign in the army.

An old friend of my father, a distinguished military officer, recommended my being sent to spend the intervening time in Germany, there to lay the foundation of a military education, which might be of service to me in after years. Accordingly, I was started in a steamer to Hamburg, whence, for the first time master of my own actions, I was to find my way to Hanover where I was duly expected at a species of military academy kept by an officer formerly, I believe, belonging to the German Legion. To effect this object, my indulgent father had given me more money than I ever dreamt of so soon possessing; and as I paced the deck, and jingled the gold in my pocket, I fancied myself a *millionnaire* about to create no little sensation in the weak minds of the foreigners among whom I was to sojourn.

On board the vessel I had a small division allotted to me for a bed, much resembling one of the shelves in my dear mother's linen-closet, and in which I could neither lie down nor sit upright; while above me I had a Russian officer who suffered dreadfully with the *maladie de mer*, and a German underneath who never got out of bed during the whole time we were on board, and did nothing but drink schnapps, and follow the example of my northern friend in the upper shelf. This was rather too much of a good thing, and as I suffered none of the inconvenience to which my fellow voyagers were martyrs, I remained on deck and picked out the softest plank I could find for a couch, decidedly preferring a bivouac in the open air to the vile atmosphere below.

Most persons have been on board a steamer, and all steamers are very much alike, the same rumbling, grumbling, and groaning of machinery; the same thump, thump, thump of the paddle-wheels; the same abominable smells in every part of the vessel; and the same odd-looking people among the passengers. In due course of time we arrived at Hamburg, where I remained a few days, and then proceeded to my destination.

Hanover is, or was in my time, a dull place, inhabited by dull people, who gave dull parties, with a great deal of ceremony, and very little to eat. But there was a nice little theatre there, and the music was superlatively good. This is generally the case in Germany, the musical taste of the people being too well cultivated to allow of their listening to any but the best performances.

Lounging in the shops the greater part of the day, and then passing the evening at the opera, were the usual expedients which the young Englishmen there made use of to kill the time, which their friends in England no doubt persuaded themselves was devoted to their studies. I think it a decided mistake for parents to send their sons to any establishment on the continent. They can learn nothing there that could not be taught them better at home, and the terms of these places are generally very exorbitant.

I think nothing more desirable for the young military aspirant than travel on the continent; but his time would be better employed in making a tour, with a competent person to attend him, than wasting it at any species of academy, and the cost would be decidedly less. Indeed I have heard the observation from many young men whom I knew at Hanover and have since met, that the bills sent home to their friends from Germany, greatly exceeded what a first-rate education would have cost at either Oxford or Cambridge.

I learned to smoke the Meershaum, to shoot with the rifle, and use the broad-sword,—accomplishments in which the Germans decidedly shine. Their rifles are first-rate, but their fowling-pieces are contemptible; they are vilely made, and shoot most execrably. It is an extraordinary thing that the Germans cannot use the fowling-piece with any degree of skill, while as rifle shots they are unrivalled. I made the acquaintance of the jagers at the Jager-hof at Hanover, and was always invited to join the great boar hunts in the royal forests, which are really worth seeing.

In about a year and a half from the time that my name was placed on the Commander-in-chief's list for an ensigncy, I was recalled home, and shortly afterwards came the long wished-for missive from the Horse-Guards, addressed to Ensign G——, of the 31st Regiment of Foot, then in Bengal. Never shall I forget the feelings with which I rushed up to my mother's room to show her the important document. I felt I had my foot on the first step of the ladder by which I was to mount to the summit of my ambition. Had I been made a peer of the realm I should not have felt prouder than I did with that letter in my pocket; and when my dear father bade me remember that the Duke of Wellington's career commenced in India, and smilingly asked why mine should not be as glorious, I thought not of the weary years that must roll by, ere I could hope to command even a company. I was an ensign, that was certain:—and that I should shortly be a colonel, was equally so. Eight years seemed almost an eternity in those days—quite the transition from youth to age;—yet eight years have passed away, and I look back as if it were but yesterday, at my boyish dream, and wonder what my feelings then would have been could I have foreseen that I should only have mounted the second step of the ladder in so great a lapse of time.

Fortunately the letter came after breakfast, or I certainly should have eaten none that day. I rushed at once to my tailor, and gave him no peace until my uniform was sent home. On the day it came there was a review in Hyde Park, and I thought it would be a glorious opportunity of shewing off my fine feathers; but I had to send for the man of stitches to instruct me how to put on my sword-belt and tie the sash, which were quite beyond my comprehension. Down I marched at last, feeling very uncomfortable in my new habiliments which, with a total disregard of comfort, I had ordered to be made exceedingly tight. If I was not the finest fellow there that day, I thought I was, and that was quite sufficient for me.

I took good care to salute every private I saw, after the manner common to young ensigns; and returned home quite satisfied with myself, and the appearance I had made, nothing doubting but that I carried with me the hearts of most of the young ladies who had been unlucky enough to see me.

A few days afterwards I had a far better opportunity of again indulging the world with a sight of my fine clothes. I was presented to his late Majesty, and had the height of my vanity gratified by being saluted by the Life Guardsmen on the stairs. I ran up and down two or three times to make them do it again, and returned home in a transport of delight, which I believe none ever felt but young ensigns under similar circumstances. I thought that every one at the levee had had his eyes fixed on me, totally forgetting that had that been the case, instead of an Adonis, they would only have seen a short, stout boy in a red coat, with nothing very remarkable in his appearance in any way.

I could not bear my plain clothes after the regimentals, and longed to enter on my new duties; so before the usual two months' leave of absence was expired, I reported myself to Captain B., then commanding the depôt of my regiment at Chatham garrison.

On joining the depôt I was at once handed over to a serjeant to be initiated in the mysteries of the drill of a recruit. This was a horrid bore.

## RECRUITS' DRILL.

The commencement was absolutely intolerable, and rather disgusted me with the reality of my new life. It really appeared so ridiculous for one who certainly imagined himself rather a distinguished person than otherwise, to be with two or three other ensigns stuck on the right of a squad of very awkward recruits, dressed in precisely similar jackets to theirs of coarse red cloth, and leaden buttons, with a hectoring serjeant making the most of his brief authority in such words as these:—

"Now, Mr. A, head up, if you please, sir.—Shoulders square, Mr. B.—Now, if you please, gentlemen, attention—stand at ease—*'tion.*—Now, gentlemen, if you please.—To the right.—Too quick that time, Mr. A.—To the right—face!—As you were! When I says as you were, I means as you was," &c. &c. &c.

This, however, did not last long; and the best thing a young man on joining can possibly do, is to give his whole attention to it, and he will soon be dismissed as perfect. It is a most necessary ordeal, although young ensigns generally think otherwise; for no officer can possibly reprove an awkward man in his company with any effect when he is known to be deficient himself.

I should recommend young men who may be gazetted to regiments in India, not to join the depôt, but to obtain leave from the authorities at the Horse-Guards at once to join their regiments. This I believe is always granted on application, as well as the government allowance of £95 passage money, paid to the ship master with whom they may make a bargain for a cabin. For this sum a passage may always be obtained with a separate cabin. The masters of ships ask more, but none of them will refuse it if they find they cannot persuade you into increasing the amount. Chatham is decidedly anything but a good school for young men. The officers are mostly strangers to each other: here to-day and gone to-morrow; and, belonging as they do to so many different regiments, will not be bothered with offering advice to young men, which probably would not be taken when they are not attached to their own particular corps. This is different when the regiment is joined. There is a species of freemasonry among the members of every corps, which will insure to the young recruit the advice of experienced heads, whenever he is disposed to seek it, and very often without his doing so, if his seniors take an interest in him, which they assuredly will do, in every gentlemanly and well-disposed young man.

There is a subject connected with his voyage to India to which I would direct the particular attention of the young recruit. I mean the selection of his outfit. The persons who make their livelihood by providing these things, invariably persuade their victim that he will require hosts of articles which he hardly ever heard of before, or knows the use of, independently of giving him at least three times the proper quantity of those which are really necessary. And what with soldering up in tin all those things which he is to find so indispensable, and various other expedients which they will use to swell out their bills, they generally make the outfit amount to pretty nearly the price of the first commission, and in some instances I have known it exceeded. I will now give a list of what is necessary for the comfort and respectability of a young officer proceeding to join his regiment in India:—

One regimental coatee

One pair epaulettes

One blue frock coat

One pair shoulder-straps

Two shell jackets, of cashmerette, or other light materials

One cloth ditto

Materials for another of cloth, not made up

Four pair cloth regulation trousers

One sword

Two sashes

One buff belt with breast-plate
Two forage caps
One chaco
Two sword-knots
One pair of pistols.

I have not mentioned linen, people having different ideas respecting the quantity which will be necessary for four or five months' wear. Perhaps six-dozen shirts, the same number of socks, and four dozen of towels will be enough. A few can always be washed on board, if your man collects water in buckets whenever it rains, which it frequently does about the line most heavily.

The full-dress coat is seldom worn in India, not more on an average than four or five times a-year. One, therefore, is quite sufficient. Not so in England, where the officers dine in their full-dress coats every day, wear them at many parades, and mount guard in them. Under these circumstances, it is of course necessary to have two; one for all-work, and another to wear on state occasions, when young ladies are to be captivated at balls, dinner-parties, &c.

Nor is the blue frock much worn. In some regiments officers never appear at parades in them. The shell-jacket is worn at all parades and duties of every kind; and, as red cloth is very expensive in India, and difficult to be obtained, I recommend four to be taken out, three made-up, and materials for another. At mess, officers generally wear white jackets. These should not be purchased in England. They are to be obtained quite as well made in India, at a quarter the price, and there is generally a regimental pattern, which must be strictly adhered to. White trousers should also be obtained in India, the cost of them there, made of American drill, which is the material always worn, is about six or seven shillings a-pair. Those furnished by English tailors will not stand three washings, which indeed is the case with all articles made of linen cloth.

The natives wash clothes very differently to the method adopted in England. The dhobies, or washermen, have a large board, purposely made very rough on one side. This they take down to the river, and after wetting the clothes, beat them upon it. Indeed they often beat them between two stones. Cotton cloth stands this pounding pretty well, but linen is destroyed at once.

I would not recommend portable chests of drawers to be taken out. They may be purchased in Calcutta for about £3, equal to those which cost £10 at home. The bullock trunks also are made too large in England. No Indian bullock could carry them when full. I have seen some on so large a scale, that I am sure it would be beyond the power of the wretched beasts commonly procurable to carry even the empty boxes. A very good pair can be bought in India, with straps complete, for about £1 10s. I suppose a London trunk-maker would charge £5 for inferior trunks. Neither should expensive dressing-cases, or writing-desks be taken out; they invariably go to pieces during the hot winds. No man ever thinks of shaving himself in India. A native barber comes every morning to perform that necessary operation for a mere trifle per month. The best description of writing-desk is a portable one of Russia leather. A canteen, or portable iron bedstead, should never be taken out. They are totally useless, and from their weight a great incumbrance and expense; yet the outfitter will assure the young officer that they are absolutely indispensable, and that he could not possibly do without them. The consequence is, that nearly every ensign that joins takes out one of each, and after probably paying about as much as they originally cost for carrying them hundreds of miles about the country, finds he can never make any use of them; that nobody would take them even at a gift, and that the cheapest plan for him to have adopted at first, would have been to throw them overboard during his passage out.

## FIRE ARMS.

A pair of pistols may be considered a most necessary part of an officer's outfit. They should not be too long and heavy. Barrels about six inches in length, and twenty to twenty-four bore, I should recommend as the best size. They should also be furnished with spring-hooks at the side to fit on a belt, and the triggers should be made to pull exceedingly light, or they never can be used with accuracy. A general fault with pistols is their being made so excessively stiff in this respect that it is impossible to keep the sight on the object when firing. They ought to be purchased of some eminent gun-maker, on whose respectability dependance may be placed.

Nothing of this kind should ever be selected from the stock of Birmingham rubbish with which outfitters are in the habit of tempting young and inexperienced persons going out. They are generally got up in a very showy manner, in smart cases, often with German silver furniture, in order to catch the eye. Avoid them —they are often unsafe, and never to be depended on. If the outfitters can make them go off their hands, they do not care if they never go off afterwards; and certainly in many cases it would be desirable if they did not, they being more likely to injure the persons firing them, than any one else.

As every military man should know something

of the manufacture of fire-arms, I should advise those who desire information on the subject, to purchase " Greener on Gunnery." Mr. Greener I believe is a gun-maker at Newcastle, and evidently a most scientific and superior man. I was greatly gratified by the perusal of his book. It affords abundance of most important information, and will enable any man carefully reading it, to defend himself from the chance of being taken in by any of the many thousand unsafe and rascally-made guns and pistols (often bearing the names of our best makers) which are weekly turned out at Birmingham, and not only distributed over all the kingdom, but shipped out to the colonies, where of course a reference to the person whose name they bear is out of the question. Many, for want of ability to detect the imposition, have purchased them and lost their hands, or been otherwise seriously injured by using such vile imitations. Strange that people, for the sake of a little gain should, with a total disregard of the fatal consequences to their fellow-creatures, continue to manufacture and proffer for sale these regular man-traps.

A short period disgusted me with Chatham garrison. There was no way of killing time, but strolling down the town, and then strolling back again, or playing at billiards from morning till night. Nothing in the way of getting up a flirtation with a pretty girl at the pastry-cook's, or any other little amusement of the kind was known of. These young misses who are generally so susceptible in country towns, were here so accustomed to see soldiers at every turn, that they absolutely thought nothing of them: a fact decidedly any thing but gratifying to the vanity of the young ensigns, who had persuaded themselves that they were not to be looked upon with impunity, whereas they were reluctantly compelled to admit that the belles of Chatham had seen, and not fallen in love at once, or in fact ever dreamed of such a thing. Even the servant maids did not cast a second look when the irresistibles passed the door steps they were scrubbing.

## CHAPTER II.

Author embarks for India—Shipmasters on shore different persons from shipmasters at sea—Reflections on leaving home—Story of a shark—The flying Dutchman—Catching turtle in a calm—First sight of India—Pilot comes on board—Anecdote of a tiger—Shooting at Diamond Harbour—Arrival at Calcutta—Indian servants—Indian cities—The beggars — Fakirs — Marriage processions — Hospitality of the European residents of Calcutta.

THREE other young men who had been appointed to my regiment determined with me to cut the dull life which we spent at Chatham, and to go out to India at once. We accordingly applied for leave to find our passage out to join the regiment, thus making a pleasant party together. This was granted, and we came to terms with the master of a ship of 800 tons burthen, then lying in the West India Docks. After some bargaining, we each obtained a separate cabin for the government allowance, and in the month of October, 1836, embarked at Gravesend, nothing doubting but that we were going to the finest country in the world, and that we should find the master the same liberal, off-handed, and good-natured fellow he appeared on shore. In fact, we considered ourselves especially lucky in finding such a man, whose sole pleasure, he informed us, consisted in trying to make his passengers happy and comfortable in his ship, and to enliven the tedious monotony of the voyage by every means in his power. They were his friends, his guests; of course, he could not afford to take them quite gratis, but he made nothing by them—not he; no, the pleasure of having friends around him at sea amply repaid him for any pecuniary loss.

No sooner did the Captain come on board than the anchor was hove up, and we proceeded to Portsmouth, where the remainder of the passengers were to embark.

The night they came on board we had a severe gale of wind, and were obliged to put back to Ramsgate. The first part of our voyage was thus rendered very unpleasant. Most of the passengers were very ill, and I almost regretted the exemption from sickness which I enjoyed. Few of the others could leave their cabins, and the dinner and breakfast tables were deserted and unsocial. If I shut myself up in my cabin, I was disturbed by the moanings and complaints of my neighbours; and if I went on deck every body seemed to think me in the way. The sailors were scarcely recovered from the drunkenness in which their last few days on shore had been spent. All was bustle and disorder. Nothing seemed to be in its right place, and it was with some difficulty I pushed my way to the poop, which was the only place in the ship not occupied by dirty half-drunken sailors in noisy debate,—ropes in indescribable confusion,—trusses of hay,—hencoops, pigs, sheep, and passengers' luggage.

Never until now had I thought seriously of the home and friends I was leaving—perhaps for ever. I leant over the taffrail, and as I watched the glimmering lights on shore, from which we were fast departing, and listened to the moaning of the wind, and the dashing of the waves under the counter, I contrasted the cheerful fire, and my own snug room in my father's house, with the dreary sea prospect, the comfortless cabin, and monotonous imprisonment which awaited me here. How I longed for one look at the book of futurity!—what was to be my fortune in the far country to which I was going! and how many of those dear friends to whom I had so lately bid adieu, and whose kindness since my earliest remembrance now rose in review before me, and forced itself on my recollection,—might I have seen for the last time!—The glad tones of welcome with which they would have hailed my return to my native land would be perhaps, ere then, hushed in the silence of the tomb!

A few days of fine weather completely altered the face of things. Those who had been sick crawled out of their cabins, and seemed to recover their health and spirits almost by magic, and we now began to find out something of each other's characters. Some of the passengers were very agreeable people, and seemed by their sociability desirous of making the time we were to be together, hang as lightly as possible on our hands. Others, as is always the case, were inclined to make themselves particularly disagreeable and were disposed to quarrel with everybody. These we soon sent to Coventry, and they formed a party of themselves, and tormented each other the whole voyage. We invented a variety of means to enliven the tedium to which we were exposed—got up a weekly paper, and acted plays, the ladies assisting the latter by manufacturing the dresses, and wigs.

In spite of all these contrivances, however, the time passed slowly enough, and we found our liberal friend, the master, not quite the sort of person he had represented himself. The table was kept in the most stingy and niggardly manner, and the wines were execrable.

Sometimes we used to catch a shark, or harpoon a dolphin, as he played under the bows; a good deal of fun took place in overhauling the locker of the foremost fish, as the sailors call searching out what he has in his stomach. We found all sorts of odd things that had been dropped from the ship days before. There is no doubt that these voracious sea monsters will follow a vessel hundreds of miles on her voyage. The sailors believe that when any person is sick on board they never leave it, knowing from a peculiar instinct, when the malady will prove fatal, and the body be thrown overboard. The truth of this I do not vouch for; but the sailors will enforce their narratives with many examples which are startling, if true. I heard a story which is curious, and I do not think unlikely. The narrator once sailed on board a ship, he said, in which there was a very near-sighted passenger who always wore a pair of gold spectacles. He had forgotten to provide himself with a second pair, before he left, and being a man of nervous temperament, he was perpetually worrying himself with the idea that by some accident or other he should lose the only ones he had during the

## STORY OF A SHARK.

voyage, and thus be left for some time in a most unpleasant predicament, not being able to see a yard before him without the assistance of glasses. Many and dire were the accidents which he was sure would happen to him in the state of semi-blindness to which he would be reduced, when the barnacles were gone. In fact, he would be afraid to venture on deck, being certain to walk over-board, or fall down the companion-ladder; and how he should ever get into the boat which was to take him on shore, when the ship arrived at her destination, he knew not.

One day they were becalmed near the line, and a large shark was seen by the officer on watch just under the stern. All the passengers, our near-sighted friend among them, rushed aft to see the monster taken, a baited hook having been immediately put over-board. In the scuffle which took place, every one striving to get a good position, down dropped the spectacles from his nose; the shark seized the glittering prize, and as if satisfied with his acquisition retired under the counter refusing the most tempting baits that were successively offered him during the day. Towards evening a breeze sprung up and away they went at nine or ten knots an hour. The nervous man was now in the situation which his morbid fancy had so often presented to him, and the first part of his presentiment having come to pass, he felt like a doomed man, and seemed to await the fulfilment of his destiny, which, he had persuaded himself, was either to break his neck, or be drowned. He locked himself up in his cabin, became moody and reserved, and busied himself with arranging his papers, and making various preparations for his end. The captain, and others became seriously alarmed, and attempted to rally him from this monomania, but all to no purpose; he shook his head mournfully when they attempted to laugh him out of it, and solemnly made answer, that time would show he was a doomed man.

The wind about the line seldom lasts long, and after five or six days' fair sailing during which they ran eight or nine hundred miles, the favourable breeze died away,—the heavy sails again idly flapped against the masts,—and again the usual listlessness which attends a perfect calm at sea crept over the minds of every one on board. One of the midshipmen who had gone aloft to see if he could descry a sail or any thing else on the vast expanse of water, on which they lay like a log, sang out, that a shark was close to the vessel. Again every body was on the *qui vive,* a hook was soon baited and thrown over, and this time greedily snatched at by John Shark. He was soon hauled on board, and the business of searching his locker commenced with the usual curiosity. The first thing they pulled out were the gold spectacles! They were speedily taken down to the hypochondriac below, and the change which the sight of them made on him was miraculous. He felt, he said, just what a man would, who with the rope already round his neck, is reprieved at the gallows' foot, and at once shaking off the fit of despondency and apprehension which had clung so closely to him, he joined heartily in the laugh which his former fears now raised among his fellow voyagers. I give this story as I had it and leave the reader to judge for himself how much of it is true. In a shark which we caught, we found a newspaper of later date than any we had on board, and which was dried and read by all of us, not having been at all injured by its adventures. It must have been dropped from some other ship, and swallowed by our eccentric friend.

When off the Cape of Good Hope, we were continually honoured with the company of numberless Cape pigeons and albatrosses, which seemed delighted beyond measure with us, and followed in our wake for many days. We caught a great number, some of the latter birds measuring as much as twelve feet across the wings. They are easily taken with a baited hook, kept on the surface by a piece of cork and thrown over the stern when the wind is light. The greedy birds soon take the tempting *morceau* (generally a piece of pork fat) and are hauled instantly on board. It is singular that they immediately become sea-sick, cannot rise from the deck, and are altogether the most helpless creatures imaginable. The sailors, who willingly eat anything in the way of fresh meat at sea, made a variety of dishes of their flesh. One of these, a species of stew, I was foolish enough to taste, and certainly never shall forget the atrocious flavour of the mess, which was devoured with much apparent *goût* by these amphibiæ.

We doubled the Cape without seeing the flying Dutchman, who the sailors say is always cruizing in these latitudes. Our old boatswain told some very terrific stories about him, all of which he would swear were true; and I dare say he had told them so often that he believed the greater part himself.

"One night," he said, "when he was a youngster on board an East Indiaman, a severe gale sprung up off the Cape. The wind was so strong that two men were obliged to be stationed aft, to hold the captain's hair on his head, and the night was so dark that the look-out men were obliged to feel if their eyes were still in their sockets. The hands were sent aloft to double reef the topsails, but somehow or other the reefs came undone as soon as they were tied. Suddenly they were hailed by a ship just under their bows, sailing with every stitch of canvass spread, directly in the wind's eye; and he could distinctly see, from where he lay on the topsail yard, her crew lying idly about her decks, and smoking their pipes with the utmost *nonchalance,* seeming to think the hurrican every good fun. The hull, rigging, and the crew themselves shone like phosphorus in the gloom around; and, by the lurid glare of the lightning, he could observe that they were clothed in the broad bottomed breeches, and sugar-loaf hats, which are represented in the old Dutch prints. On she came, as if she intended running them down; but her hail, which was repeated three times, was not responded to by the Indiaman. Suddenly, as a collision seemed inevitable, she disappeared, but instantly afterwards was again seen astern, sailing away in the very teeth of the storm. This was the flying Dutchman; and no sooner had she gone by than the difficulty of reefing the topsails ceased, the gale abated, and before morning they were again ploughing their way, with a fair wind, across the trackless ocean."

Had Vanderdecken's attempt at communication

been acknowledged, the boatswain informed us, the ship must have been lost; the only thing that saved them being the refusal of the captain, an old stager, to answer the hail. Why the sailors have this belief I cannot make out, as I never could get it satisfactorily explained. I questioned the ancient mariner very closely on this point, but he could not enlighten me, being himself perfectly satisfied that it was so, without troubling himself about the reason.

In the Bay of Bengal we met with light winds, and were once becalmed for a whole fortnight. During this time the sea looked like an immense mirror, and numberless turtles were seen basking on its placid surface, their back shells being quite dried by the heat of the sun. It was intensely hot; but we youngsters having no fear of *coup de soleil* or fever before our eyes, spent the greater part of the time in one of the boats, sometimes harpooning, and sometimes turning these Aldermanic delicacies. To effect the latter purpose, it is necessary for the boat to be propelled by a scull astern, in the quietest manner possible, while the person who performs the operation kneels in the head of the boat. When the turtle is within reach, he gently leans over him, and seizing the flippers on the farther side, suddenly turns the animal on its back. It is then perfectly helpless, and is easily lifted into the boat. Care must be taken not to go near its beak, for they bite most ferociously. When we took them on board, the sailors used to cut their throats, and drink the blood, affirming that it tasted like new milk; but I suspect it must have required a very strong effort of the imagination to arrive at this conclusion.

The delay we met with here, rendered the voyage very tedious. It is when the long-wished-for port is within a few days' sail, that people become excessively impatient; and the slightest delay is almost insupportable. At last, however, land was in sight, and certainly it was not the sort of land I expected to see. Instead of the delightful country I had pictured to my mind's eye, of verdant meadows, and tree-crowned hills, I saw nothing but a long low bank of sand, stretching away on either side as far as the eye could reach. I was sadly disappointed. Can this desert, I exclaimed, be the fairy East I have read of in romance?—How different is the reality!

Towards morning a pilot came on board from one of the Company's brigs which we fell in with, and we now began seriously to think our voyage at an end. We passed Saugar Island, famed for the number and ferocity of its tigers, and presently a canoe filled with natives came alongside, who proffered for sale straw hats, and various kinds of what they call fruit in India, but which we at home should term very bad vegetables.

The daring of the tigers about Saugar, when pressed by hunger, almost exceeds belief. The following singular adventure with one occurred to the brother of an officer in my regiment. He was in the Company's service and was proceeding on board one of the government steamers up the Sundabunds, with a party of sepoys, in charge of treasure. One night when they were anchored as usual in the middle of the stream, he was awoke by a great scuffling and tumult on deck just over his head. Thinking that it must arise from an attack of robbers, who had made an attempt to possess themselves of the rupees under his charge, he seized his sword, and springing from his cot, rushed up the companion ladder. No sooner did his head appear above the combings of the hatchway, than he received such a smack on it as completely deprived him of his senses, and sent him head foremost down again rather quicker than he came up. On recovering himself, he found a tiger had boarded them, and that after killing his bearer and two sepoys, and giving him a facer that would have done credit to Tom Spring, he had again betaken himself to the water, and swum ashore, apparently quite satisfied with his own performance. This is one of the many well known instances of their boarding boats, and killing, or carrying off a portion of the crews.

We were all impatience to get to Calcutta, as the wind was in the favourable direction up the river; but the pilot assured us it was impossible for him to take the ship up during the night, as it was against the Company's strict regulations. This it appears was a ruse, to obtain possession of some of our loose coin, as we were informed shortly afterwards, that the pilot would take the responsibility of violating the regulation on himself, if a certain sum were handed over to him as a consideration. The cunning fellow knew well enough that our impatience would not allow us to resist the imposition, and, accordingly, we subscribed enough among us to induce this conscientious functionary to proceed.

We got up to Diamond Harbour that night when we came to an anchor, and early next morning, before the tide served, F— and myself bribed some natives to put us ashore as we were impatient to commence operations against the Indian game. We, of course, shot at every bird we saw; and returned on board as they were heaving up the anchor, with a motley collection of Paddy birds, and mynahs, having enjoyed our sport very much; but were rather disgusted when laughed at for a couple of griffs, by all the old hands on board for wasting our ammunition at such carrion.

No sooner had we landed at Calcutta, than we were surrounded by a host of servants in search of situations, all fighting among themselves, and disputing with the most vehement gestures, accompanied by volleys of abuse on their respective mothers and female relations of every degree. Most of these worthies spoke English, and extolled themselves, and ran down their rivals in such terms as these:

"Master, want good servant? not d—n rascal like that fellow there; I very good man. This servant for master — 'spectable servant: same, like self."

"Master not take that man; he one d—n thief: master look here, plenty good character got;" another would cry, displaying a number of small pieces of paper, signed by different officers. One of these I had the curiosity to examine, and found the following attestation to the honesty of the candidate for my service:

"The bearer of this, one Khoda Bux by name, is the most infernal scoundrel under the sun; he attached himself to me on my first landing, and cheated me in every way he possibly could for a week. On my finding out, and dismissing him, he had the impudence to ask me for a character; and I have therefore given him this, hoping it may be of service towards giving any gentleman, to whom he may offer himself, an insight into his character.

"A. B., Ensign,—Regt., N. I."

With some difficulty we forced our way through these harpies, but not before we had knocked one or two of the most troublesome down. No sooner had we got rid of them, than we were surrounded by a host of palanquin bearers, who fought desperately among themselves for the honour, or profit of carrying us in their palanquins to our destination. We settled this dispute by picking out the four best, and then kicking the others away; and with four umbrella bearers, with their chattahs, who had, unasked, attached themselves to our persons, running alongside our palkees, we were trotted off to Spence's Hotel, where we intended taking up our quarters.

Next morning we reported ourselves to the Brigade Major at Fort William, and then proceeded to deliver the letters of introduction with which we were furnished to the respective gentlemen whose addresses they bore. These are technically called in India tickets for soup, as the bearer of one is invariably asked to dinner; which is the only attention that people generally feel themselves called upon to shew. Having got through these preliminary engagements, we proceeded to the China bazaar, our palanquins being attended by numbers of itinerant dealers in pen-knives, razors, old books, and various other commodities, the excellence of which they most vehemently expatiated upon, as they pressed the articles upon our notice.

Arrived at the bazaar, we were pounced upon by a fat Bengalee, who seated us in his shop, and provided us with a cheroot, and a glass of brandy and water each before he unfolded his commodities for our inspection. A whole posse of rival dealers, meanwhile, besieged the door, and endeavoured to persuade us by the most flattering description of the excellent quality, and cheap prices, of their own wares, to change our quarters. As we did not want to purchase anything in which they dealt, and only came to the bazaar in order to pass away some part of the day, we did not think it necessary to do so, but remained in our comfortable situation, purchasing nothing, but amusing ourselves with a scene so new to us; our fat friend looking on us with a rather blank countenance, when we assured him, in the blandest tones, we were much obliged to him for his attention, and enjoyed his cigars very much, although we did not happen to want any article in the heterogeneous collection his shop contained.

When we got tired of this, we again packed ourselves in our palkees, and proceeded to the bird bazaar, where we purchased a monkey each and then returned to our hotel. I retired to my room to dress for dinner, and was just washing my hands when the door was thrown open, and a respectably dressed native, followed by about twenty others in various costumes, walked in. On inquiring rather sharply the cause of this intrusion, the leader of the gang threw himself into an attitude, and addressed me in the following words:

"Master, new gentleman, just come—master want servant—plenty too much very bad man in Calcut. I one highly respectable man—I hear master one very great sahib and want servant. I go, save master trouble, and bring servant for him. This fellow," pointing to the first on the list, "is master's kitmutgar; next fellow, master's washman. Two, three day, master buy horse, that fellow take care master's horse; next fellow cut grass for same; and me," laying his hand on his heart, and making a low bow, "I master's head man; I take care of master's clothes, keep his money, and do every thing for him, master have no trouble at all."

I could scarcely help laughing at the fellow's impudence, and found it difficult to get rid of him, until I assured him if he did not speedily make his exit, and take the followers he had so benevolently provided for me with him, I should be at the trouble of kicking him and his tail out of the house. When he found I was in earnest, he departed; and I understood afterwards played the same game successively on my three brother officers, but without succeeding in seducing them to take him.

Calcutta has been called "*The city of palaces,*" but why I cannot conceive. There is nothing grand or striking in its appearance whatever. The houses inhabited by the European residents are large, and some of the shops in the principal streets good, but not to be compared with those of London. I imagine it has acquired the name by comparison with the other cities and towns in India; and certainly they are immeasurably inferior in every respect. People in England have an idea that such places as Agra, Delhi, Benares, and a few others, must be on a very magnificent scale; but they only differ from other towns by having more inhabitants, and being infinitely filthier. All Indian cities are very much alike.

There is generally a long narrow street, with shops on each side, which is called the bazaar. These shops are occupied by dealers in grain, copper-smiths, cloth-merchants, and manufacturers of sweetmeats, of which the natives are immoderately fond; and the manufacture of which, therefore, is a profitable business.

The swarms of flies about these shops would beggar description. They are bred in millions, and are a most intolerable nuisance. At Delhi, the air seems absolutely alive with them. The sweetmeat-makers are always dirtier than any other class of natives; and to see them prepare their dainty wares is absolutely disgusting. This operation is always performed in public, and it is difficult to imagine how the natives, after witnessing it, can make up their minds to eat these mixtures of dirt, sugar, and perspiration.

The bazaars are always thronged with people; some purchasing goods, but more for the sake of gossiping, and seeing what is going on. A great nuisance in such crowded places are the Brahminee bulls. These brutes, which belong to nobody, and are worshipped by the natives, generally take up their quarters in the grain-bazaar, and help themselves out of the various baskets which are exposed for sale by the dealers, who dare not refuse them food. So bigotted are the people, that they would assuredly murder any one who injured them; and the fact of one being killed by a European or Mussulman, would be enough to excite a whole province to rebellion. They are turned loose, when young, as offerings to Brahma in return for any benefit which his godship may be supposed to have conferred upon any individual or his family; such as recovery from sickness, the birth of an heir, &c. &c. They get very fat, and are often exceedingly fierce and dangerous.

Numbers of fakirs or beggars also are always to be met with in the bazaars. These scoundrels are generally those who, disliking work, take to begging as an easier mode of getting their livelihood. Their faces and bodies are marked with different kinds of paint, which gives them a hideous aspect. Their hair is commonly plastered with cow-dung and ashes, and altogether they cut a most disgusting figure. If denied the alms which they solicit, or rather demand, often in a most authoritative manner, they vent their disappointment in torrents of abuse and curses. The natives generally are induced by fearing the consequence of a refusal to give them money, although they assuredly never would do so from any feeling of charity. I have seen another description of fakirs who are in the habit of mutilating themselves in various ways. Some hold their arms uplifted and hands clenched so long above their heads that the sinews become stiffened, and they cannot move them down or in any other direction, and the nails of their fingers having grown through the backs of their hands, protrude three or four inches from the flesh, more like the talons of some wild beast than the nails of a human being. Some stand on one leg for a number of years, never changing their position, until by disuse they can no longer move their limbs. I saw a man near Ghazeepore standing in this position under a peepul tree; and the natives about the place informed me that he had not moved for fourteen years. When I saw him, his limbs were quite contracted, and were evidently of no more use to him than if they had been made of wood. He stood like a statue, and took no notice of any one, great as was the number of those who stopped to look at him. He asked for nothing; but I suppose he was fed by the natives of a village adjoining, who no doubt esteemed themselves highly honoured by the circumstance that so holy a man had taken up his quarters so near them.

Marriage processions are another abominable nuisance in these crowded thoroughfares. The bride and bridegroom, both children, are carried about in palanquins covered with red cloth or other finery. They are accompanied by a band composed of natives, playing on wind instruments of the harshest and most discordant tones, followed by the eternal tom-tom or drum, and aided by the vocal assistance of every person engaged in the procession. These yell forth the nuptial hymns at the pitch of their voices, and each I fancy with his own version of the words, imagination coming into play when memory fails. The din may be conceived better than described. I have known the natives, after they had been engaged in a festival of the kind to be so hoarse from their efforts that they could hardly speak for a week.

The other parts of all Indian cities are alike. They are composed of a mass of mud huts, built in most admirable disorder, and in which live the natives with their dirty wives and filthier children; pariah dogs and pigs making up the rest of the population.

Some of the higher casts of natives are excessively clean in their persons and houses; but they are seldom seen, as they live as privately as possible, and do not generally like any one whom they consider of an inferior race to themselves to go near their dwellings, or come in contact with them in any way.

At Calcutta. I was invited to many parties, and met with various very pleasant people. Among these I shall never forget the hospitality and kindness which I experienced from Mr. A——n, one of the partners of the agency-house, to which I carried out letters of credit. This gentleman continually invited me to his house, and really had he been a near relation of my own, instead of a perfect stranger, he could not have shewn me more attention. He is the prince of good fellows, keeps a splendid table, and never is so happy as when doing the honours of it to his friends. Long may he live to adorn it, and enjoy the large fortune which his industry has gained him!

## CHAPTER III.

March up the country—Shooting on the road—Sight of a tiger—Killing a bear—A shot at a fakir—Making bear's grease—A sirloin of bear's flesh—Pariah dogs—Jungle fever—H.M. 49th Regiment—Dâk travelling—Arrival at Dinapore.

AFTER ten days' stay in Calcutta, we resolved to proceed and join the regiment then stationed at Dinapore, nearly five hundred miles up the country. Accordingly, F. and I determined to march by land, while our brother officers made up their minds to go by water up the Ganges, on the left bank of which Dinapore is situated. We anticipated no end of adventures with wild beasts on the road, which lies, in many parts, through thick jungles and forests. Bullets were cast by wholesale, and every thing prepared to give the gentlemen as warm a reception as possible, should we be so lucky as to fall in with them.

The hot season was at this time approaching, and the sun during the day was most oppressively powerful. We, therefore, determined to move at night, and accordingly one evening after dining, and spending a few jovial hours with our friends, who wished us every success on our trip, we mounted our horses, and started on our journey. It was one of the moonlight nights which are so bright and beautiful in India, so clear, that one could have read the smallest print; while the trees with which the road was lined, looked as if they were tinged with silver. Our baggage had preceded us the morning before, with orders to halt at Augaparah, about ten miles from Calcutta, which is the usual march.

Our people were at the place appointed, and they had prepared our beds in a half ruinous bungalow on the side of the road. We slept soundly enough, being tired after our ride, and the jollification which we had enjoyed at Calcutta before we started; so soundly, indeed, as not to be disturbed by the jackals, which we afterwards found a most intolerable nuisance. They howl in a most unearthly manner, and generally keep it up all night, while they prowl about an encampment in search of prey. The next morning a servant of mine who spoke English, and who therefore was our factotum, came and informed me, that this was the last bungalow we should see for many days' march, and that, therefore, it would be impossible to proceed without tents, which we had never thought of. He, of course, according to the invariable custom of the natives, never said a word about them until we had left the place at which such things were procurable. This was pleasant. There was no help for it, however; go back we must and purchase tents, notwithstanding our dislike at retrograding, after once making a start, and that with the certainty of being laughed at by our brother subs for our griffishness in going without such necessary appendages.

While we were discussing this point, we were surprised by the arrival of a detachment of European soldiers, who appeared on the ground, and made preparations for encamping. These we found out were a number of volunteers from the 20th Regiment, proceeding to join the 49th at Hazareebaug. They were under the command of a Captain T., of the 26th Regiment, a very excellent fellow, who, on hearing of our dilemma, most kindly pressed us to make use of his tent, a very large one, and by no means to think of going back. He was alone, he said, and would be delighted with our company. This obliging offer we closed with at once, and afterwards felicitated ourselves not a little on our luck in falling in with the detachment. We soon discovered that, from our complete ignorance of the country, the manners of the people, and the language, we

## USURERS. 45

should have been exceedingly uncomfortable, and exposed to every kind of annoyance from the rascality of the natives, who had hired themselves to us as servants with the intention of making a pretty sum by cheating us on the road. They did not seem at all to approve of the plan of joining the detachment, and some deserted that night, it not being worth their while to proceed, now we had some person with us who was aware of the tricks generally played off on griffs. The greater number of servants who get situations with young men in Calcutta, will only serve them during their griffinhood. When they find they can no longer rob with impunity, they leave their situations, and go in search of another fresh hand, whom they pluck in the same way. In this manner, these scoundrels often manage to amass a considerable sum of money, when they set up the trade of usury, lending money at the rate of twenty-four per cent interest, to young officers and others. They have often been the ruin of thoughtless youths who, had they not fallen into such hands, would probably have become ornaments to their profession. We rather rejoiced that the vagabonds had made themselves scarce before they obtained an opportunity of robbing us to any extent.

We proceeded on our march with great glee. The soldiers were as fond of sport as ourselves, and went out with us every day to beat for game. We had capital shooting at partridges, pea-fowl, hares, snipes, and innumerable wild-fowl, and we were rather an acquisition to the detachment, which otherwise would often have been on short commons: very little in the eating way, being procurable at the wretched villages through which we passed. After ten or twelve days' march, the country presented a wilder aspect, and became jungly. Tall thick grass, interspersed with stunted bushes, began to take the place of well cultivated fields, and we now anticipated falling in with nobler game than we had as yet been able to find.

We observed that the few villages which we passed were stockaded round, to prevent the incursions of the wild beasts at night. Several deer and wild hogs crossed our path and were shot. One evening, the camel drivers came running into camp in great alarm. They had taken the camels to drink at a jheel\* a little way in the jungle, when a tiger made his appearance for the same purpose on the other side. They, of course, at once took to their heels and could not be persuaded to go back; but having pointed out the direction in which they had seen the beast, we loaded our rifles, and, accompanied by about a dozen volunteers from the men, started in chase. When,

\* A lake or marsh.

however, we arrived at the jheel, he had taken his departure. We found the prints of his feet in the loose sand, and followed them some distance into the jungle; but, as night was fast closing in, and it was already so dark that we could hardly see ten yards around us, we judged it prudent to return. Our friend was prowling about the camp all night, and in the morning we found he had killed a bullock belonging to one of the hackeries,* which had got loose from its fastenings, and strayed away a short distance in the jungle to graze. F— and myself remained behind next morning, and had another hunt for the tiger, but were again unsuccessful.

On arriving at the village of Ragonathpore, a number of the natives came to our tents, and complained most bitterly of the conduct of two bears, which had taken up their residence in a cave in a mountain close to the village. The brutes had killed some, and mutilated others of the inhabitants, who had fallen in with them while collecting fire-wood, or searching for honey, bees' nests being common in the jungle, and of these the bears are immoderately fond. I saw one poor wretch who had been frightfully mangled. He had been on the mountain, he said, searching for honey, when the bear suddenly rushed on him

* Indian carts.

and tore the scalp from the top of his head with his claws, and otherwise severely wounded him. This had occurred about a week before our arrival.

No sooner had we swallowed our breakfast, than the guns were overhauled, and put in readiness for instant service. We sent for the head man of the village, who soon collected fifty or sixty of the natives provided with tom-toms,* and various other noisy instruments to act as beaters. A party of the more respectable inhabitants said they would accompany us; and they accordingly came armed to the teeth with spears, swords, and shields, and some few with bows and arrows; others, in the excess of their zeal, had brought out matchlocks, but they seemed to have such a vague idea of how they were to be used, and carried them in such a dangerous manner, generally pointing at somebody's head, that I decidedly objected to this part of the armament. I had, moreover, no great opinion of the steadiness of our new allies; and even allowing that they did not shoot any of us by accident on the way to the hill, I felt pretty certain that on the least alarm in the jungle, a shower of balls would be sent in every direction but the right one, and that probably some of the beaters would be shot, of which of course we should get the credit. They were accord-

* A kind of drum.

ingly though unwillingly left behind. Some of the soldiers obtained a few spears in case we should come to close quarters; and after a great deal of noisy discussion on the part of our beaters, as to the nearest route to Bruin's residence, we started. On arriving at the foot of the hill, we made the natives sit down while we ascended to reconnoitre the ground. We found a second hill behind that which the bears were said to frequent, and in a ravine dividing the two their foot-marks were plainly discernible. From these we could form a very good idea which way they were likely to take when forced to break cover. There we determined to take our stations in order to cut off their retreat from a large thick tract of jungle, beyond which, it was evident from the trail, lay a favourite resort of theirs.

A sergeant who accompanied us was placed at one end, while F— and I took up positions about a couple of hundred yards apart, in the ravine, where two well beaten tracks intersected it, both evidently favourite runs. I had a double rifle with me, and was attended by a servant, on whom I thought I might depend, with another double gun loaded with ball, which he was to hand to me as a reserve, in case I should not dispatch the brute with the first piece. A corporal of our party, an intelligent fellow, was now sent back with orders to take the beaters round to the other side of the hill, and extending them across the whole breadth of the jungle, with which it was covered, to beat directly down on us and to order them to sound their trumpets, and beat their drums with all their might on the way, so as to drive every animal concealed therein from his lair. He accordingly departed on his mission, and I posted our native allies who were most noisy subjects, and a great nuisance, where I thought they would be least in the way, earnestly entreating them to be as quiet as possible.

I had just returned to my station when I heard our beaters on the top of the hill, and a deer brushed past me, but so suddenly that I could not take aim at him. The plot now began to thicken, and shortly afterwards a bear made his appearance in the ravine, about eighty yards to my right, and I was in hopes he would come my way, but was disappointed. He turned down towards F——'s station, and I heard both his barrels go off, and shortly afterwards another shot from the serjeant at the end. The beaters were now half way down the hill, and the noise they kicked up was certainly sufficient to have driven all the beasts out of the country.

I was just moving down to F—— to hear

what he had done, when I heard a tremendous rustling and cracking of jungle in front of me, and out came an enormous bear, right on the path on which I was standing. We were within five yards of each other, and the brute seemed staggered by the suddenness of the unexpected encounter, and for a moment inclined to turn tail. The infernal din of the musical instruments behind him, however, prevented that, and he made a rush at me. I had taken aim at his head the moment he appeared, and as soon as he moved on the open path, I let fly and dropped him on the instant; he gave one ferocious growl and expired. I had shot him exactly between the eyes, and being end on, the ball had passed through his head into his body, playing no small havoc with his intestines on the way.

On looking round for my servant, he was nowhere to be seen, and on calling out to our native friends I found they were missing also. I climbed to the place where I had posted them, and from thence had a good view of them running as hard as they could lay legs to the ground in the direction of their village; my aid-de-camp, with the reserve gun and all my ammunition, being of the party. They had evidently bolted the moment the bear made his appearance, and the young sportsman may take a hint from this never to expect a native to stand by him when there is any danger, or he may be left in an awkward predicament. It is seldom, indeed, that wild animals of any size are killed by a single ball, and the plan which I always afterwards adopted, was to take my reserve gun from the native, and place it on the ground close by my station, always taking care also to have some spare balls and powder in my own pocket. It was then immaterial whether the nigger ran away or not. F—— soon came down on hearing my shout, and from him I learned that the other bear had got off, but he thought he was wounded. We determined therefore to follow him, and see if we could not dispatch him also.

On arriving at the sergeant's post, he informed us that he had fired without effect, and that Bruin had gone up the hill again, finding so many enemies on his path. While here, we heard a shout from the hill, which had a perpendicular descent on this side, of about twenty or thirty feet. On looking up, we saw Bruin plainly enough standing on his hind legs in a menacing attitude, and one of the beaters seemingly paralyzed at his appearance close by him. We could not fire, the man being between us and the bear, but on our shouting to him he seemed to gain confidence, and swinging his iron-bound

## AN ACCIDENT.

latee\* round, he gave the brute a rap on the head with hearty good will. Bruin's frontispiece, however, was thick enough to allow him to receive a much harder knock with impunity, and he advanced evidently enraged, and with his mind made up for mischief. The native retreated backwards to the verge of the cliff, and, seemingly having completely lost his recollection in the present danger, in spite of our shouts of warning, made another step, and in an instant was over the precipice.

We ran to the spot and found him very seriously hurt by the fall; he had also received an ugly scratch from the bear and was unable to speak. The other beaters soon crowded round the place and said he was dead: but I found he had life enough in him to clutch pretty firmly some rupees which I put into his hand. We sent him home, and then wished to proceed to the next jungle to which Bruin had been tracked. No persuasions, however, would induce the natives to go in again; they had had enough of it. In vain we offered them double pay, and pointed out that the accident which had occurred was entirely owing to the man's own folly. Had he moved on one side out of the way, instead of attacking the bear, and then tumbling down the precipice in his fright, we could have shot the

\* A long club of the solid or male bamboo.

animal from where we stood. All would not do: one man had been killed they said, and though it was very good fun for us to kill the bears, they did not see any fun in being killed themselves. It was useless to attempt to draw the jungle without beaters, so we were at last reluctantly obliged to give it up, abusing them most heartily for their cowardice.

On looking round for something at which to discharge my rifle before departing, I espied what appeared to be a monkey seated on a rock at the top of a small hill behind us. He was a long way off, but I thought I would try a shot. Accordingly I fired, but the ball struck short, and the figure did not seem to take any notice of the report. In order to rouse him from his apathy, I elevated rather higher to allow for the distance, and firing the other barrel, sent its contents this time close under him. He was now evidently alarmed, and starting to his legs, began to run for it. To our astonishment, we now perceived that what we had taken for a monkey was a man, and I had very narrowly escaped sending him to his last account. I was completely taken aback on finding my mistake, and asked the natives why they had not told me it was a man at whom I was firing. They coolly answered that they did not wish to spoil my sport, and that I might fire all day at the individual if I wished. He was a holy man, they said, who always lived on that rock, and never ate or drank anything; and of course being so sacred a personage, he could turn my bullets aside at his pleasure, and I should, therefore, never be able to hit him. I was quite as well satisfied that I had not succeeded in my attempt, and his invulnerability on this occasion doubtless added no little to the high opinion which the natives had already formed of his sanctity.

When we arrived in camp with our prize, we were received with great acclamations by the female part of the population of the village, who crowded round the monster which was carried on a pole by ten men. They called down blessings without number on our heads for destroying such a scourge to their country, and ended with asking for a buxees, or present of money for their good wishes. We were pleased with our sport, and by the distribution of a few rupees made them equally so with us; and they abused their lords and masters heartily when we told them that we should certainly have killed the other, but for their want of courage. I set one of the soldiers, who had been a butcher in his youth, to skin the brute, which we found was six feet nine inches high, when standing on his hind legs, measuring from the crown of his head to the heel. Another of the men, who had been a hairdresser, collected all his fat to render down into bear's-grease. He presented me with a quantity when it had undergone the necessary preparation. It was genuine no doubt, and that was its only recommendation, for it was nasty stuff, and I should have been very sorry to put any such filth on my head. The soldiers determined to eat the flesh; and as we had often heard of bears' hams being such delicacies, we thought we too would try him. Accordingly, a most noble sirloin was cut out in professional style by our friend the butcher, and handed over to our cook for the morrow's dinner; orders being given him, however, at the same time to have something else, in case of its not turning out quite as good as we anticipated. The soldiers had a fine feast the same day, and assured us that it was delicious; and we certainly began to look forward to enjoying a treat. The morrow came, and in our impatience to taste the rarity, we ordered dinner an hour earlier than usual; and, after talking about it all day, we at last heard the joyful announcement that it was ready. We sat down, and the sirloin, which we had already eaten in imagination half a dozen times, was brought in. It looked very well, but on taking the first mouthful, I looked at F—, he looked at T—, and he without saying a word, seizing the long-expected delicacy, threw it out of the tent. The flavour was horrible : I never tasted any thing so abominable in my life. It was fortunate that we had something else for dinner; for eating the bear's flesh was out of the question. We had, however, a hearty laugh at the way in which we had been taken in, and were greatly amused at the sight of a party of hungry pariah dogs, which had collected round the smoking joint outside. Each in turn seized it and attempted to carry it off: but each was forced immediately to drop it with a burnt mouth, snarling and fighting with the rest for a bite at the corners, and places where it was getting cool. In the midst of their strife, a half starved mangy-looking brute that had carefully kept aloof from the engagement, and maintained an armed neutrality by shewing his teeth at every dog that came near, watching his opportunity, made a dash at the savoury bait, and regardless of its being scalding hot, bolted off with his prize at a pace that gave his outwitted companions little chance of regaining it, although they all joined most hotly in pursuit.

The skin of the bear was a great prize, being very black and handsome. I sent it to England afterwards, and on my return had the satisfaction of seeing it in excellent preservation, formed into a rug for my mother's dining-room.

A few days after this event, my sport was spoiled by my being seized with a violent jungle fever, attended with delirium, and other most dangerous symptoms. In consequence of the report made to Captain T. by the apothecary who attended the detachment, he sent me by dâk to Hazareebaug, where proper medical assistance could be obtained, that being the only chance of saving my life. There was no palanquin to be had, but the bearers made up a sort of a vehicle with my charpoy* and some bamboos, which answered the purpose. We were several marches distant from the station, but my sturdy bearers trotted along famously, being promised double buxees; and in about eighteen hours I was set down at the bungalow of the senior assistant surgeon of H.M. 49th Regiment, at Hazareebaug. I had never seen or heard of this gentleman before in my life, but his kindness and attention could not have been exceeded, had I been his brother. I was very ill, almost at death's door, when I arrived. He immediately had a room in his house got ready, and I was put to bed, and the most active measures at once put into operation. I was bled, leeched, and blistered, until I appeared

* A rude Indian bedstead.

but a shadow of my former self; nothing but this active treatment, I heard afterwards, saved me, as I had inflammation of the brain from *coup de soleil*. For a long time I was delirious, and my life was hanging on a thread; but, thanks to God, and a good constitution, a favourable turn took place, and I was in a fair way of recovery.

One morning when in this situation, I was surprised by a visit from Colonel Bartley, then commanding the 49th. He had heard that a young officer had been brought into the station ill, and like the good Samaritan determined to do all he could to alleviate his sufferings. He had been down several times to inquire how I went on; but until this morning it was not considered prudent by poor Robertson, who attended me day and night, that I should see any one. No sooner had Colonel B. come in, than he shook me by the hand, and in his kind tones assured me how delighted he felt on finding that the unfavourable symptoms had passed off. "And now, my dear boy," said he, " a little ride every morning and evening will help mightily to set you on your legs again. I have two carriages, one of which I never use, so I beg you will consider it quite at your service, and it shall come down and fetch you every day, as soon as the doctor will let you go out." Such conduct as this speaks for itself:

it needs not, therefore, that I should make further comment on it. Poor Bartley is dead now, and although he was beloved and revered as a father, by the whole regiment, none of them can regret him more than I do. Poor Robinson, who attended me so constantly and kindly, and who, with God's assistance, was the principal cause of my recovery, is also now no more. He was a very old assistant surgeon, and was appointed shortly after my illness, as full surgeon of the 9th, and died while with that corps at Chinsurah, of cholera.

When I began to get out a little, I experienced the utmost kindness from the officers; they all seemed like a set of brothers; a more pleasant or united corps it never has been my luck to fall in with. They have lately distinguished themselves very much in China, and with such a commanding officer, and such a feeling as there was throughout the regiment, it never could be otherwise.

I remained at Hazareebaug about a month, when being convalescent, and anxious to join my own regiment, I took leave of my kind friends, and having bought a palanquin, and laid a dâk, started on my journey one evening, and arrived at Dinapore on the second day afterwards. This dâk travelling is very easy, and, when the journey is not long, not unpleasant, although some people exclaim bitterly against it. It must certainly be exceedingly disagreeable to those who cannot sleep in a palanquin, and this is a general complaint; while on the contrary, I have always found it exceedingly difficult to keep awake. When about to make a journey of this kind, application is made to the post-master of the station, whence it is intended to depart. This must be done some days before the intended journey, as he has to send letters to the head men at all the stages on the route, to warn them to have in readiness eight bearers for the palanquin, one or two torch bearers, and as many banghy burdars as are ordered. These banghy burdars carry two petarrahs* in slings, at each end of a bamboo, and run along-side the palkee. Of course, their number is determined by the quantity of baggage to be carried. People seldom take more than a few clothes, and plates, and dishes, with eatables sufficient for the journey. Two are, therefore, the usual number accompanying each palanquin. When the dâk is properly managed, they time the progress of the traveller so exactly, that the bearers are always found waiting at the appointed places; and they relieve the old bearers, and trot away with the palanquin with scarcely any delay. When a stage is completed, the relieved

* Small boxes.

bearers expect a small present for themselves, in addition to the expenses of the dâk, which must always be paid beforehand to the post-master. The amount of buxees is determined by the manner in which they have carried the traveller on their stage. They generally get eight annas,* four annas, or nothing, according to their pace. The set of eight bearers, which is the regular number, continually relieve each other on the road, as only four at once carry the palanquin. The usual rate of this mode of travelling is three and a half miles an hour, day and night, and costs about eighteenpence a mile.

On arrival at Dinapore, I was very kindly received by all the officers of my regiment, who, from the accounts they had heard of my illness, never expected to see me there. I was still very weak, and the commanding officer kindly informed me, that I need not do duty until I had recovered my strength. I dined at the mess the day I arrived, and as I was still quite bald, my head having been shaved during my illness, I have no doubt I was the most singular looking recruit that had joined the regiment for some time.

* An anna is of the value of three-halfpence English money.

## CHAPTER IV.

Sporting at Dinapore—Snipe shooting—Tiger hunting—Indigo planters at Tirhoot—Anecdote of a lion—A tiger hunter in an unpleasant situation—Jungle fowl—Runaway elephants—Jungle bees—Catching wild elephants—Sagacity of elephants—Hog hunting—A pig-sticking griff—Bobbery pack—Treatment of dogs and horses—Syces and grass-cutters—Horse-dealers—Races—Sailing on the Ganges—Anecdotes—Sporting griffs, &c.

DINAPORE is a very bad station, very hot, and but little shooting in the vicinity. There is a jheel, however, on the opposite side of the river in which I have bagged a good many snipe. In case any of my readers should ever be stationed there, I should recommend them to cross the river opposite the church, and after passing a nullah\* which lies about a mile inland to continue their route straightforward for about five miles, when they will find another nullah, with rushes on each side. Let them turn up the left bank of this, and shooting their way about three miles, cross the nullah, which is not, in some

\* A small river.

places, more than three or four feet deep, and shoot back on the opposite side. It is not a first rate snipe jheel, but a good shot may make a very fair bag during this walk—from fifteen to sixteen brace. Beyond this nullah again, about a mile, there are some small jheels, which generally are full of snipe; but they are not extensive. They may be shot over in about two hours. I used generally to leave them alone until I had beaten both sides of the nullah, and then adjourned thither to finish my day, and these jheels being the haunt of all the snipes which are driven from the first place, they were then very plentiful. But although Dinapore has no good shooting close at hand, it is a station most favourably situated for the tiger shooter, being not more than ninety or a hundred miles from the Terai, where the best tiger shooting in India is to be had. It is of no use to go out after tigers until, the hot weather having commenced, most of the jheels and ponds of water left by the rains are dried up.

Tigers are naturally of a hot constitution, and the quantity of flesh which they devour makes them more susceptible of thirst than most other animals. While these pools and jheels are full, therefore, the tigers are dispersed all over the country; but when they become dried up, it is only necessary to beat the jungle in the vicinity of nullahs, or places which are never dry, and the tigers will all be found congregated there, while miles of ground, where there is no water obtainable, are often beaten by parties, who go home and complain there are no tigers left in the country; when, had they only hunted in the vicinity of water, they would have had good sport.

The first trip I ever had with a regular tiger shooting party, was from Dinapore. A gentleman who was in the habit of going out invited F. and myself to join him in a month's excursion, to which, of course, we most readily assented. Having obtained leave, therefore, we laid our dâks to Betteah, seventy miles from Dinapore, where we were to meet Mr. J., and one morning, directly after muster, stepped into our palanquins, and started on our journey. We went on well enough until we arrived at Mazufferpore at 12 o'clock that night. Here the bearers put us down, and informed us there was no relay waiting. Fortunately, the post-master of this station had formerly been doing duty with our corps as assistant surgeon, and as he was a very good fellow, we determined to go to his house and knock him up to see if we could, by his means, be spared farther delay on our journey. He informed us there must have been some very bad management on the part of the post-master at Dinapore, as he had received no notice of a dâk being required, and he was quite sure there was none laid. He, therefore, recommended us to have our palanquins brought to his bungalow, while he ordered beds for us to sleep there, and in the morning he would do his best to forward us. This was pleasant, after having paid our money for the whole distance to a government functionary; but there was no help for it, and we accepted our friend's kind offer with thanks. Next morning he gave us a lift in his buggy for twenty miles to Mooteearree, where he informed us a most capital fellow, Mr. T——, an indigo planter, resided. Some shooting might be had at snipes and wild fowl, and while we were engaging ourselves in that way, our palanquins were to be brought on by a number of bearers who would take us then to Peprah, some thirty miles farther. A princely fellow, indeed, we found Mr. T. He was delighted to see us, and the snipe shooting was first rate. I never saw such thousands of these birds in my life. The marsh was very extensive, and they got up in clouds, so many at once, that we hardly knew which to fire at. After this capital sport, we returned to dine at T's hospitable mansion, and that evening took leave of our liberal host, who warmly pressed us to stop the month out there.

We arrived next morning at Peprah, and with

the assistance of another indigo planter there, obtained a fresh supply of bearers to take us to Betteah, where we found our horses waiting. Mr. J. had gone on, leaving word for us to join him at Boggah, some twenty or thirty miles farther. We breakfasted at Betteah, and there mounted our nags and proceeded, but lost our way; and after riding about the jungle all day got into Boggah late at night, tired to death, and hungry as hunters. From this place, we found Mr. J. had again moved on; and consequently we could get nothing to eat. His encampment was eight miles further on in the jungle; our horses were knocked up, and we had nothing for it but to bivouac under the trees for the night. In the morning we rode on, and met Mr. J. just going out. He had killed a tiger the day before, and we found our howdah elephants all ready with fourteen others for beaters. The howdah generally is made something like the body of a phaeton. The sportsman sits in the front seat, and on each side of him, are two divisions for the butts of his guns, the barrels of which rest upon a kind of splash board in front, in which grooves are made to admit them. There is a door on each side of the front seat, which is secured by strong iron hooks. In the seat behind, a native is placed, whose business it is to hold an umbrella over his master's head. Some people have their guns loaded by these men; but I should decline trusting that operation to a native. The howdahs thus described are liable to many objections. The doors weaken the frame very much, and frequent accidents have occurred to sportsmen, when leaning over the front piece to get a shot, by its giving way, and precipitating them into the jaws of the infuriated animal.

An accident of this kind occurred to an officer, when lion-shooting. The front of his howdah gave way, and he fell close to the lion, which immediately seized, and walked off with him. I do not exactly know how he was rescued from this perilous situation; but he used to tell the story at mess, and amuse everybody very much by the quaint way in which he related it. " I was worse off than Daniel," he used to say, " for Daniel was in the lion's den,—but by Jove, I was in the lion's mouth."

When in Calcutta, I saw another officer who had been carried off by a tiger, and was only saved by his extraordinary presence of mind. I believe he also fell into the jaws of the brute by his howdah giving way; but however that was, the tiger seized, and carried him off. His friends were afraid to fire at the beast, lest they should kill the officer. Fortunately, he had a brace of pistols with him; and, while the tiger was taking him away, he drew one and discharged it into his body. The only effect which this produced, was to make the savage beast clench his teeth still deeper into the flesh of his victim, and growl with rage. But one chance now was left, and our friend was resolved to make the best of it. By getting firm hold of the long hair about the neck of the animal, he managed to work himself round in the tiger's mouth, so as to be able to feel with his hand where the heart of the monster beat strongest, and firing his remaining pistol in that place, killed him on the spot. His friends attracted by the shots came up, and found him senseless, and the tiger dead. The gentleman recovered, however, but was always lame, from the dreadful lacerations he had received.

The best howdahs are those made without doors, of a strong wooden frame, covered with buffalo hide. It is easy when mounting to step over the side, and this plan precludes the possibility of the front coming out. Four guns are necessary for the howdah, two on each side, and it is most convenient to have them of the same bore. I have found great trouble when a tiger was on foot, and I was loading in a hurry, from the bullets being of different sizes, getting one now and then stuck half way down the barrel, with no means at hand of drawing it up again, and thus having one or more guns rendered useless, at the very moment when they were most required. A rifle is a most useless weapon for tiger shooting. It takes so much longer to load than a smooth bore, without any corresponding advantage, as all tiger shooting is at close quarters. If the brute charges, he is seldom fired at a greater distance than twenty yards; indeed, in most places the jungle is so thick that it would be difficult to see even an elephant at a greater distance.

After breakfast, we stepped into our howdahs, and forming the fourteen pad elephants in line, began to beat the jungle. We disturbed numbers of different kinds of deer, wild hogs, pea-fowl, partridges, and various kinds of game, including many jungle fowl. These beautiful birds are our common fowl in the wild state, and are the gamest looking birds I ever saw. I used frequently to fancy myself in an English farm yard, when I heard them crowing in every direction round our tents. We passed many fresh carcases of bullocks and deer, in the high grass, which had been killed by tigers; but we were not successful in finding any of those beasts that day. The fact was, we were too early in the season, and we therefore determined to shoot every thing that came in our way, instead of attending to the usual restriction of tiger parties —which prohibits the shooting anything but the nobler prey.

The next day we killed a boa constrictor, twenty two feet long; and towards the evening J— who was in the centre of the line, got a shot at and wounded a tiger in some high grass. The brute took to the left where F— was stationed; but the moment he broke cover, F—'s elephant bolted. F—'s attendant, by some carelessness or other, at this moment allowed the umbrella to drop on the stern of the elephant. The terrified brute I suppose thought it was the tiger that had sprung on him, and giving the unfortunate umbrella a kick with his hind leg sent it flying into the jungle. During this confusion, the tiger made his escape, and the evening closing in, we were obliged reluctantly to leave him; it was however only for a time, as on a subsequent day J— killed him, and found he had hit him on the former occasion upon the hip. The place had festered, as is usually the case when these brutes are wounded, and he would no doubt have died from its effects. It is no trifling affair when an elephant takes it into his head to run away, which they often will on the sudden appearance of a tiger. It does not much matter in grass jungle, but such an event has occurred to me twice when in a thick tree jungle. The first time, the animal bolted just as I was leaning over the howdah to get a shot, and wheeling suddenly round, I very narrowly escaped being thrown out. He went off at a rattling pace, breaking down all the trees in his way. I was in a very dangerous predicament, being elevated among the branches, some of which I expected every moment would dash my brains out. At one sweep all my guns were knocked out, and I then got under the seat of the howdah, which being fortunately very strongly made, stood the blows pretty well.

When the animal was at last brought up by a large cotton tree against which he got his head, but could not break down, I emerged from my place of shelter, and found the front of my howdah much damaged by the blows it had received from the branches of the trees, during our unmanageable charger's run. To regain my guns was not very easy, and occupied me a long time. The elephant had got over nearly a mile of ground before he was stopped. The gun which I was in the act of firing when he started, I was obliged to let fall at that moment, in order to save myself from being thrown out. It had fallen in a marshy place, and the barrels were stuck nearly two feet deep in the soft earth, both locks being on full cock. Strange to say, neither had gone off with the concussion of the fall. We were not very successful with the tigers on this trip, but shot quantities of deer, hogs, and small game.

I should recommend any person starting from Dinapore to send his elephants, horses, tents, in fact, his whole establishment to Betteah, and go to that place himself by dâk, taking care that his arrangements are made rather better than mine were in this respect. From Betteah, he should march as far as Muttanpore, which he can do in four days easily, before he attempts to beat for tigers; but when there, he will find ample work for a week. Many tigers have been killed at Muttanpore, and there are always some about that part of the country. I once fell in with four lying together in the grass at this place. From Muttanpore he should cross the Gunduk river to Busei, and in the Jhow jungle there, he will assuredly find two or three. I was once beating this jungle when mounted on an elephant belonging to the Rajah of Betteah, and the mahout* informed me that some time before, Colonel W— of the European Regiment, a famous tiger shooter, had been on his elephant in the same place,

* A native who has charge of the elephant and who manages him on all occasions.

and that in two mornings he had killed nine tigers.

At Busei there is a *gwallor*, or herdsman, by name Ramdeall. This fellow knows the haunt of every tiger in the neighbourhood, and for a buxees will not fail to point out where sport may be had. It is necessary in this place, and in fact all over the Terai,* to carry a couple of blankets in the howdah, in case of being attacked by the jungle bees. These little wretches are the most ferocious animals I ever saw. Should one of their nests, by any accident, be overturned they sally out in swarms, and attack both elephants and men. The only plan to adopt, is immediately to wrap oneself up in a blanket, through which they cannot sting. I once met a gentleman who informed me he nearly lost his life for want of this precaution. The bees attacked him in millions, and stung him so severely, that he was for a long time confined to his bed. I once was out when a wounded tiger upset a nest of these pestilent little insects. They, as usual, attacked every body, and drove our whole line back in disorder; but I was fortunately provided with a covering to defend myself from their tiny weapons. Several of the elephants, however,

* The name of an immense tract of jungle which is a notorious resort of tigers, and other kinds of wild beasts.

became outrageous, and a friend of mine was thrown out of his howdah. Some time elapsed after we had rallied our forces at a distance, and returned to the spot, before we could find him in the jungle. Happily he was unhurt.

From Busei, it will be advisable to go on up to the bank of the river, which swarms with alligators to Bowar. When I was at this place, I met a European gentleman who had obtained a grant of land from government, and proposed cultivating it. He was at this time living in a tent with a few servants; but how he has succeeded in his speculation, I know not. He appeared a very agreeable person, and happy to give every information in his power. On a second occasion, when I was in the Terai, I again met him, when he informed me that he had built the walls of a bungalow, and had only to roof it in, when one night a herd of wild elephants came down, and before morning destroyed all that his people had been for months employed in erecting. At Bowar there are always a few tigers, and the deer are innumerable. They start up in the grass jungle, at almost every step the elephants take.

About nine or ten miles from Bowar, is a nullah, called the Boggalee Nuddee. At this place, I remember once being out with a party when we killed six tigers in one afternoon. We encamped at a place called Teekah. There is a Nepaulese village here, the inhabitants of which are very civil and obliging. They are great hunters, and often kill the largest animals, even tigers, in their nets. The nets which they employ are made very strong, and a considerable extent of jungle may be encircled with them. When this has been done, a number of large dogs are turned in to beat out the wild animals that may be inside. These, on rushing violently forth, are of course entangled in the nets, and the natives, who remain outside armed with heavy iron-shod clubs, soon close round them, and knock their brains out, before they can free themselves from the toils. I was much amused with the activity of the fellows whom I saw engaged at this work. They also use the pellet-bow, with great accuracy of aim. These bows, with the exception of the string, are precisely like those used for arrows. They have a double string, and in the centre a small cradle is made of platted hemp, or something of the kind, to receive a ball of clay baked in the sun. This, when the bow is drawn, is discharged with great force. I met a man one day in the jungle, who knocked some pigeons and other birds off the trees at astonishing distances with one of these machines.

## WILD ELEPHANTS. 77

The village of Teekah is somewhat beyond the boundary marks of the Company's territory; which is denoted by a chain of pillars of brickwork running across the Terai. On one of these, near Bowar, appears the name of the famous Lieutenant John Shipp* cut out with a knife, or other instrument.

In the Terai are many wild elephants. I never fell in with any myself, but have frequently seen their tracks. Many are caught by the natives employed by the Rajahs residing near that part of the country. A gentleman whom I met at Goruckpoor, informed me he had been out several times and seen many taken. He described the mode of capture, as follows:—In the rainy season, at which time the wild elephants are very numerous in the Terai, the hunters go out on two or three very powerful tame elephants, provided with some strong ropes. There is no howdah, or pad of any kind on their backs, so that it requires some degree of skill for the riders to hold on. They then go in search of a herd, and as soon as they fall in with one, the tame animals mix themselves up with the others as if they belonged to them. They manage to keep clear of the old elephants, which are very

* Who so much distinguished himself in the Nepaulese war and elsewhere.

cunning and powerful, and then manœuvre so as to cut off any young one which may have strayed a short distance from the others. As soon as they have so far succeeded in their intention as completely to surround him, they wait as if grazing until the remainder have got some distance off. The young one, meanwhile, seeing companions so near him takes no notice of the departure of the main body.

When these have got sufficiently far away, the hunter who is mounted on the nearest elephant advances close to his victim, and throwing a rope in the manner of a lasso, entangles him in its coils. The other end of the rope being fastened about the elephant which he rides, he at once starts off, and drags the unwilling captive after him. Should he struggle much, the other hunters close round, and throw additional ropes until he is completely entangled and escape is hopeless. He is then taken to the camp and secured with ropes; and, in a very short time, by kind usage, is domesticated. They only try this plan on small elephants. The old ones, in the wild state, are very fierce, and more than a match for half a dozen of those which are domesticated. The large ones are generally taken in pitfalls, numbers of which I have seen in Terai. Sometimes also they are entrapped by means of a female elephant fastened in the jungle with a broad trench dug round her. The wild males, hearing her cry, come to the spot, but the trench stops them. No elephant is able to get across any chasm that is wider than he can stretch his fore feet over. They cannot jump; and if the place is deep, they never attempt to cross, knowing well that if they be once in a hole, their immense weight makes it extremely difficult to get out again. They remain on the edge of the trench, therefore, paying their *devoirs* to the lady at a distance. Meanwhile, the hunters creep in among them, and fasten on their legs strong chains, which are secured to trees in the neighbourhood, or to thick posts driven into the ground. When they find out the snare, they are at first outrageous; but the natives picket a tame female elephant on each side of them, which alternately fondles and beats them into good behaviour. Being kept without food for some days, their spirit is broken, and they soon allow a mahout near them, who for a short period feeds and caresses them, and then mounting on their necks, renders them meek, gentle, and willing slaves.

It is astonishing how docile these animals become after being for some time domesticated. The mahout, his wife, children, and the elephant all form one family. The elephant has his dinner of large cakes of unleavened bread, prepared for him at the same time as his ruler, and they all eat together. I have seen a mahout and his wife go to the bazaar to make their daily purchases, leaving their child, an infant not able to walk, in charge of the elephant. It was really most amusing and interesting to see the solicitude displayed by this gigantic nurse. As his little charge would crawl nearly out of his reach from the place where he was picketed, he would stretch out his trunk and gently lifting the infant up place him down near his feet. After playing about some time, the child got tired and went to sleep, the elephant meanwhile breaking off a green branch from a neighbouring tree, waved it gently backwards and forwards over the face of the sleeping infant, lest the flies should disturb him in his slumber. The creature might have been taught to do this, but it still proves of what extraordinary sagacity these animals are possessed.

I was once out on a tiger party in which there was a female elephant remarkably tame and sagacious. She used to come to our tents every morning while we were breakfasting to beg for pieces of bread, or anything else that was to be had. On being presented with a piece of money, she would walk off to the bazaar, and purchase sweetmeats, and wo betide the dealer if he attempted

## SAGACITY OF ELEPHANTS.

to cheat her. More than once, the mahout informed us, she had pulled the whole shop over the heads of knavish dealers who had not given her a fair exchange for her money. She would draw the cork from a bottle of beer with her trunk, no matter how tightly it was hammered down, and drink the contents. It appeared, indeed, that she was given to strong liquors; and the mahout told us she had been repeatedly dead drunk when gentlemen had given her a sufficient quantity of spirits. Two buckets full, he informed us, was about the quantity necessary to make her groggy. We did not, however, try the experiment, thinking that an inebriated elephant in a close camp would be about as pleasant a customer as a bull in a china shop.

Tiger hunting is the noblest sport in which a man can indulge, with the single exception of hog hunting on horseback. I never was fortunate enough to be stationed in any part of India where this was to be obtained, as it is of course necessary that the country should be partially open. Wherever I have fallen in with hogs, it has been in the thickest jungle, where to ride after them would be impossible. To be a good pig-sticker, as hog-hunters are technically called, a man must have a very firm seat on horseback, be a bold rider, have a strong arm, and iron nerves. His horse should be an Arab of great speed and bottom, and a fine mouth is indispensable, everything depending on the celerity with which he wheels round when the hog charges. A party engaged in this sport generally consists of three huntsmen, armed with sharp spears on solid bamboo staves, and loaded with lead at the butts. A number of natives are required for beaters; and when there is much cultivation of sugar canes in a country, hogs are generally abundant. The riders post themselves on the outside of the jungle, while the natives are sent round to drive the swine out. Little pigs are of course not worth riding after unless the game is very scarce. When a grizzly old boar makes his appearance, they are after him at once. Off he goes at race-horse speed; indeed, for the first mile it is difficult for the fleetest horse to come up with him, if he had any thing of a start. The sportsman who first overtakes him generally tries, while riding alongside of him, to drive his spear, overhanded, between his shoulders, which would kill him instantly. This is, however, exceedingly difficult to do, as the hog has a most decided objection to such a mode of proceeding, and generally turns round and charges the moment he perceives his pursuer abreast of him. This is the dangerous time, and if the horse is not instantly wheeled round out of his way, he is sure to be ripped up, and the rider will probably share the same fate. A skilful hog-hunter, however, generally manages to get out of the way, and drives his weapon into the grunter's body. This is what is termed getting first spear; and if not killed, the boar now becomes doubly savage. The other riders are by this time up, and perhaps he takes off again, when the same play is again acted, until he comes to bay, when he is soon despatched. Seldom, indeed, does a large boar fall before he has inflicted some severe wounds on his enemies. It is an expensive sport to follow, because it is necessary to have the best horses, and these are frequently done for by the hogs ripping them up, or cutting their back sinews. Moreover, the ground over which they ride so desperately, is generally much broken, and intersected with numerous ravines and hollow places, down which both horse and rider frequently fall in their headlong career. Old wells are often found in the jungle which cannot be perceived in the grass until close upon them; and they are exceedingly awkward places to tumble into being commonly very deep.

When at Dinapore, we used to get up a humble imitation of this sport by riding all over the country, and spearing every pariah dog we fell in with, and once or twice the villagers' pigs met with the same fate. These are the most disgusting animals I ever saw, and are more than half wild. I very well remember joining one day with a number of other griffs, in purchasing a couple of village pigs which, after poking them with sticks, and using various means to make them savage, we turned out and speared. On this occasion one of our number being unprovided with a hog spear, had borrowed that belonging to his chokedar,[*] a totally different kind of weapon, having a long spike at the lower end for the purpose of sticking it in the ground, which is the custom of these men. When the pigs were turned loose, our young friend in his anxiety to get first spear, using it underhanded like a knight of olden time at a tournament, made a furious charge, but missed the swine, and the spear-head being brought up by the ground, he very narrowly escaped transfixing himself on the long spike at the butt.

We also established at Dinapore what is called in India a bobbery pack. This is a pack of dogs of all sorts, no matter whether greyhounds, bull dogs, or even pariahs. Curs of every degree were admitted, and we certainly had a collection, to determine the breeds of which would, I think, have puzzled the most accomplished canine fancier.

[*] Watchman.

Every member of the Dinapore hunt was obliged to bring two dogs into the field, and we hunted every evening. Plenty of foxes were to be purchased at about a shilling a-piece; and after all the dogs had been collected and taken down to a plain near the course, and the field assembled, we used to turn them out of baskets, and great fun we had with them. Of course our hounds did not run by scent; they had noses certainly, but such as were capable of smelling little but their dinner. The bull dogs and other heavy individuals of the pack were, of course, soon thrown out, when they used generally to amuse themselves with hunting strange dogs that came near them, or baiting any unfortunate jackass or bullock which they could find grazing on the meidan.*

Well bred dogs are expensive in India, and very liable to disease. No sportsman, therefore, should be without some Treatise, from which he may learn how to alleviate the sufferings, and often, perhaps, save the lives of his faithful assistants. I think Blaine's Canine Pathology is about the best on this subject. White's Farriery is also a valuable addition to the sportsman's library. When a horse is sick in India, it is seldom that any professional advice can be obtained, and the natives know nothing of the treatment of the

* A large plain.

diseases to which it is liable. Every one, therefore, should study to obtain an insight into the subject, sufficient to enable him to be of assistance in case of need. I do not by any means recommend men to run into an extreme as many do, who are continually dosing their unfortunate quadrupeds whether they be ill or not, and are never seen in their stable but with a glyster pipe under one arm, and a balling iron under the other. But much mischief may ensue in that hot climate, when a disease, slight in itself at first, is allowed to run on; and the consequence often is, the death of a valuable animal which a little care and medical knowledge might have prevented.

In India every one who can afford it keeps several horses. The natives judge of a man's consequence, in great measure, by the number of horses in his stud. Their keep costs nothing compared with the expense in England. If one horse only is kept, two servants are required for him. The syce or groom, cleans him and runs after his master when he rides out in order to hold his horse whenever it may please him to dismount. He also carries a chowrie of horsehair for the purpose of driving away the flies with which the air of India teems, and which render a high-spirited horse very fidgetty and unmanageable by their blood-thirsty attacks.

## SYCES AND GRASS-CUTTERS. 87

It is astonishing how far these men will run alongside a horse going at a smart pace. I have frequently seen them keep up with a buggy for eight or ten miles when the horse has been going at a sharp trot. By being accustomed to this kind of thing from childhood, they are always in such excellent wind that a run of the sort requires no particular effort. The Mussulmans make much better syces than the Hindoos. They become fond of the animal which they tend, while the naturally avaricious disposition of the Hindoo, generally prompts him to steal, every day, a certain portion of the allowance of corn which, when by repeated petty thefts it amounts to a few seers,* he sells in the bazaar. The pay of a good syce is about five rupees† a month. With this sum they feed themselves, and must always be respectably dressed to attend their masters on their rides or drives.

The other servant is called the grass-cutter. His business is to go out every morning into the country, and return in the evening with a sufficient quantity of grass for the next day's consumption. This he cuts with a tool much resembling a carpenter's chisel, and after beating the grass, which is shaved off close to the roots with a fork-

* One seer is about 2lb. English weight.
† Ten shillings.

ed stick to clear away the earth, he makes it up into a bundle and carries it home on his head. The monthly pay of this functionary varies from three to four rupees.

About ten miles from Dinapore, at a place called Hadjeepore, there is annually held a large fair, to which thousands of horses are brought for sale from all parts of India. The Asiatic horse-dealers are if possible a more knowing and knavish race than those of Europe. The horses of Hindostan are often of the most vicious disposition; every species of vice that was ever known is sometimes embodied in one animal of this breed. They will attack a man open mouthed, and if they could once get him down would tear him to pieces with their teeth. It is singular that the finest looking horses seem generally the worst in this respect, and their owners use all sorts of artifices to disguise their real disposition. They dose them with opium, and, while under the influence of the drug, they appear the most docile animals in existence.

I was once taken in at Hadjeepore by one of these man-eaters, as they are called in India. Having gone down to the fair with some other officers for the purpose of looking at the horses, I was most struck by the appearance of an animal which I saw performing a variety of tricks by command of the native dealer to whom he belonged. He was a stout well made cob, and after a great deal of bargaining, I purchased him. In two or three days, the effects of the narcotic with which he had been drugged wore off, and he turned out the most ferocious devil I ever beheld in the shape of a horse. No syce dare go near him, and I had great difficulty in getting rid of the brute.

The dealers in horses have a singular mode of bargaining for their steeds. They always ask at first a most extravagant price; but this is understood by both purchaser and seller to be for no other object than to mislead the bystanders, whose curiosity may have brought them round the spot, as to the actual value set on the horse by his owner. The bargaining parties then sit down on the ground facing each other, and a horsecloth is thrown between them. Under this they both put their hands, and the rest of the negociation is carried on by signs made by manipulation under the blanket. The purchaser, perhaps, offers half the original sum demanded. The dealer strikes his breast with his hands, and looking up to Heaven, seems astonished at the other's want of conscience. A great deal of haggling on both sides takes place, and it is frequently a considerable time before the bargain is closed. When it is, however, and the customer takes his purchase away, no one but the contracting parties themselves know what has been paid for the horse.

The origin of the custom, I imagine, is this: purchasers in India generally pay according to their rank. Thus a man of inferior rank will probably purchase a horse for half the sum which a Rajah or rich native would have to pay for the same animal.

During the fair which generally lasts about a week or ten days, horse-races take place. There is a regular course, and some of the running is very good. The horses generally belong to officers and civilians from neighbouring stations, and indigo planters from Tirhoot. The jockeys are usually native boys trained for the purpose from early youth. Some of the most spirited members of the turf, however, keep European jockeys.

The running horses are commonly Arabs. Few of the country horses have speed or bottom at all to be compared with these imported animals. The East India Company, however, have of late years much improved the breed of horses, in many parts of the country, by the formation of studs for the purpose of keeping up a regular supply of well-bred animals for the use of their cavalry. The sires are all famous English or Arab stallions and the mares country bred. Many of these belong to the Zemindars*, who are in the habit of breeding horses. Their mares are covered by government horses free of any expense, but the owners are bound to present the foal when a year old for the inspection of the officer in charge of the Company's stud. If it be of a certain height, and be otherwise approved of by the inspector, he is purchased for the Company. If he be under the regulated standard he is rejected, and the Zemindar may then sell him to whomsoever he likes.

Many of these rejected colts, however stunted their growth in the first year, frequently spring up afterwards, and beautiful well-bred horses, of fifteen hands and upwards, may consequently be picked up from the native breeders at prices varying from three hundred to five hundred rupees.† When any of the full-sized horses from the stud are allowed to be sold to officers requiring them, the price fixed by government is a thousand rupees.‡ Many of the colts purchased by the Company's agents, although they may be the full height required at a year old, never attain the height of fifteen hands, which is the regulated standard for

* Farmers.
† 300 rupees, £30 ; 500 rupees, £50.
‡ £100.

the cavalry. When the horses have attained the age of four years, they are examined by a committee of cavalry officers, and those under the required size are rejected as too small. These undersized nags may be purchased by private individuals for the price of four hundred rupees each. They are capital cattle, and I think them generally able to perform more work than those of the full size. When many are rejected, and for which there are no applications, they are sold by auction, and generally fetch on an average about three hundred rupees each. They are frequently worth a great deal more, and I certainly prefer the best bred of them to the Arab, as being equal to more work and being much better horses in every way.

The Arab is certainly a delightful animal to ride in a canter or gallop; and they are such docile, quiet creatures, although full of spirit, that one cannot help liking them. They do not trot well, and when walking, trip at almost every inequality on the road, which is a great nuisance. A good horse of this breed may be purchased from the Arabian dealers, who travel about the upper part of India with strings of them, for about one hundred pounds. A very superior animal, however, will cost three or four thousand rupees*.

* £300 or £400.

The reason given for their constant stumbling in their walk, is, that in Arabia, the whole soil of the country being loose sand, they have nothing to trip them up, and consequently they get into a careless way of going close to the ground, of which habit they can never afterwards be broken.

The river Ganges at Dinapore is very wide, and sailing in pleasure boats is a great source of amusement to the officers stationed there. Some fatal accidents have, however, taken place by the boats being upset in sudden squalls which are very frequent and violent. While my regiment was there, a young officer belonging to a native corps was drowned. He, and one or two others, had had a boat of large size built, and schooner rigged, but she was very crank, and over-masted. Some of the officers of the 31st were sailing at the same time, and saw the schooner at a distance carrying a press of canvass. A sudden squall came on, and their attention was completely taken up by the management necessary to preserve their own boat from being capsized.

When the wind abated they looked about to see how the others had weathered it; but to their surprise the schooner was nowhere to be seen. When the squall came on, the sheets had unfortunately been belayed to the seats, and she immediately upset and sank. Two of the party saved themselves by swimming, but the other was drowned. Several native boats passed the place while he was struggling with the waves; but none would lend a hand to help him, little as was the effort required to save him from a watery grave.

When the men were asked why they had not saved him, they replied, "They had no orders to do so, and what was it to do with them?" The mild Hindoo as he is called, is, I believe, devoid of all feeling for his fellow creatures. One solitary passion seems to engross his soul—the love of money. Compared with the avarice of the Hindoo, that of the Jew is liberality itself.

In the rainy season, the Ganges overflows a great part of the flat country near it, and whole villages are frequently carried away by the floods. The current runs at a most astonishing rate, and I have seen hundreds of natives carried down the stream on the roofs of their huts, which being made of light bamboo and straw, float for a long time. None of their fellow-countrymen will stretch forth a hand to save these unfortunate wretches. They will sit on the deck of their boats coolly smoking their Nerreallees,* and look

* A rude hookah formed from a cocoa-nut shell.

on with the utmost indifference as ever and anon an exhausted wretch loses his hold of the piece of timber, or whatever he may have clung to in his distress, when after having been whirled round in the eddies for a few moments, the waters close over his head for ever,—perhaps not five yards from the apathetic beast who is dignified with the name of a man.

Many of the unfortunate creatures exposed to these perils, during the rainy season, while our regiment was stationed at Dinapore, were saved by one of our officers who lived on the bank of the river. Whenever any of them were seen struggling in the torrent, he instantly went out to their rescue, and brought in as many as his boat would contain. I never shall forget the return made him by a party of three or four whom he had saved. The moment he retired into his house they stole the oars and sails of the boat, by means of which he had assisted them in their hour of need. This was the gratitude of the mild and gentle Hindoo.

At Dinapore, many young men rest a few days when going by water to join their regiments higher up the country. Some curious stories are told of the sporting adventures of these youths. One remarked that he had eaten such a quantity of wild turkeys during his voyage that he had got quite tired of them. His hearers stared, knowing that such a bird is unknown in the wild state in India, and they began to think their young friend was drawing rather largely on their credulity. On a subsequent evening, however, while riding on the bank of the river, he pointed out a number of these wild turkeys congregated together. His unbelieving friends had a hearty laugh when they discovered that he had been shooting and eating the vultures, which frequent the river side in great numbers for the purpose of feeding on the dead bodies which are constantly floating down. At a short distance they have very much the appearance of turkeys.

Another party of these hopeful youths had been out shooting and killed a number of paddy birds. When they returned to their boat, they inquired the name of these of their kitmutgar.* He, not understanding English, thought they were inquiring if they were good to eat, and replied at once, "Kooch kam ke neh Sahib;" meaning to say they were good for nothing, not fit to eat. The griffs ordered them to be made into a pie for dinner; and going into the station, told their friends they had had splendid sport; and wishing to show off their knowledge of the

* Servant who attends dinner, &c.

Hindostanee name of their game, invited them to their boat to partake of the Kooch kam ke neh pie.

Another, while out shooting in a jheel with an officer of ours, happened to espy the long neck of a paddy bird erected above the rushes. At the moment he was asking his bearer what it was, the bird popped its head down again. The bearer pointing out the fact to his master, said in Hindostanee, " Goos geha Sahib," which signifies in English, "he has hidden himself." Our griff, however, thought the bearer was informing him of its species, and wishing to shoot such a large and shy bird, neglected firing at a flock of ducks which passed close by him. His companion wondering at this, shouted and pointed them out, thinking they had not been seen. To this our precocious sportsman replied, " Oh hang the ducks, man, here's a goose !"

## CHAPTER V.

Departure from Dinapore—Station of Ghazeepore—Attah of roses—Duck-shooting—Indian thieves—Showers of fish—Fruits—The pine-apple—Snakes, musk-rats and mosquitoes—Agra—The Taj Mahal—Ruins—Wolves—Famine at Agra—Sporting at Agra—Grand entertainment given by the Rajah of Bhurtpore—Ice establishment.

WE were all heartily sick of Dinapore, when in October, 1838, a sudden order arrived for us to march and relieve the 44th at Ghazeepore. This station is about a hundred miles higher up the country, and is also situated on the bank of the Ganges, but on the opposite side of the river. The women and heavy baggage of the regiment were sent up in country boats under the command of a captain, while the battalion marched by land.

There was very little shooting to be had on the

## ATTAH OF ROSES.

road, and altogether this march was one of a very uninteresting description. We arrived at our new station in about twelve days, and were generally much pleased at our removal. At Ghazeepore, which name signifies "Garden of roses," the officers live in detached bungalows, each having large compounds. This is much more pleasant than being quartered in barracks, which is the case at Dinapore. Great quantities of rose-water and Attah-of-rose sare manufactured at this station. We were besieged for the first week by numbers of itinerant dealers in these commodities. The real attah is excessively scarce. They say it requires fourteen thousand flowers to make a single drop. The whole of that which the hawkers assured us was the genuine perfume, and which the officers purchased at an extravagant price, turned out to be nothing but sandal-wood oil. Great numbers of roses are grown all about the neighbourhood, and hundreds of acres of ground are covered by the bushes. Many people who have never been at the station hearing this imagine the sight must be very beautiful. This is not the case; the flowers are all gathered during the night, the moment they burst the bud, so that a person may reside a long time in the station and never see a rose on its parent stem.

The country about Ghazeepore is flat and marshy, and is consequently very unhealthy. Thousands of every kind of wild-fowl are found on the numerous jheels in the vicinity; and the lover of duck shooting is here in his glory. Snipes are also pretty plentiful; I have frequently shot ten or twelve brace within half a mile of the barracks. I built punts on the plan of that famous sportsman, Colonel Hawker, and wrote home to England for a swivel gun, with which, when it arrived, I played no little havoc with the wild ducks, which I fancy, had no reason to congratulate themselves on our arrival. No lover of wild-fowl shooting should be without that excellent work of Colonel Hawker's, " Instructions to Young Sportsmen." The Colonel has paid more attention to this kind of shooting, than any other sporting writer of the day. All the methods which he recommends to get within shot of these shy birds, I adopted with great success. He has evidently learned them by experience, and not by hearsay.

In order to enjoy wild-fowl-shooting in India to any extent, it is necessary of course to be provided with a duck gun. One of about fourteen pounds weight, with a barrel of from four feet to four feet six inches in length, and seven or eight bore is, I think, the best size. A gun of this description can very well be discharged from the shoulder without a rest, and will carry about four ounces of shot.

Ghazeepore is a famous place for thieves. Scarcely a night passed while we were there without a robbery taking place in the barracks, or some of the bungalows. The Indian thieves are, I suppose, the most expert in the world. The quartermaster sergeant of the regiment, when we were at this station, was a very corpulent and heavy man. The staff-sergeants had bungalows, and his was situated on the left of the line of barracks: one night his house was entered by robbers, who not only cleared it of every thing portable that was lying about, but absolutely stole the very bed-clothes from under the fat sergeant himself and his sleeping family without disturbing one of them. When they awoke in the morning they were lying on the bare mattrasses. This is a common trick with Indian thieves, and the way in which they manage it, is this. The robber before he enters a house, or tent, first strips and anoints himself all over with oil,— which is done in order that in case any person should be awake and seize the intruder, he might be enabled to slip like an eel from his grasp. Thus prepared, he creeps into the dwelling as noiselessly as possible.

The nights in India are generally very close and

oppressive, and the sleep of most people, although heavy, is uneasy and disturbed. Of this the thief takes advantage. He quietly crouches down close under the bed, and with a feather gently tickles the nose of the sleeper, who, half dozing, rubs it and turns on his couch. While he is doing this, the sheet on which he is lying is withdrawn a little from under him by the thief. When he is fast asleep again, a second application of the feather causes another turn, and again a little more of the sheet is pulled away. The thief then goes on the other side, and the tickling is continued until the sheet is completely withdrawn from under the unconscious sleeper. The operation takes some time, but is always so nicely managed that I believe there is no case on record of the slumberer being awakened while the robbery was going forward.

I have heard many other anecdotes of the dexterity of thieves, which I have no doubt are authentic. One referred to the robbery of a gentleman who rejoiced in the possession of a very splendid silver mounted hookah which he was in the habit of smoking every evening. One night when on a march, and while enjoying the luxury of a most fragrant chillum,* his

* A fragrant composition of tobacco, sugar, and various spices, which is smoked in a hookah.

hookah burdar,* who was in attendance, requested leave to go to the bazaar for a short time. This was acceded to, and he departed. About the time that the chillum was nearly ended, he apparently returned, and stood with arms folded according to custom behind his master's chair. When the gentleman had solaced himself sufficiently with his favourite luxury, he threw down the snake, and the hookah was carried out in due form by the attendant, and the embroidered carpet carefully folded up and taken away. He had not been gone five minutes, when the gentleman was astonished by the sudden appearance of his hookah burdar, rushing into his tent in a state of semi-nudity, beating his breast and indulging in most noisy lamentations. It appeared that, when he departed for the bazaar, according to the custom of native servants, he had taken off the clean white clothes in which he attended his master, in order that they might not be soiled, and laid them down between the inner and outer khanauts† of the tent.

A thief who was prowling about the place saw him do this and immediately on his departure,

* Servant whose sole business it is to clean his master's hookah and prepare his chillum.
† Khanauts, walls of a tent.

clothing himself in the hookah burdar's habiliments, took his place in the tent, and possessed himself of the gentleman's splendid hookah and appurtenances in the cool manner which I have described.

Whenever people go out to dinner in India, each person is attended by his own kitmutgar, who stands behind his master's chair during dinner and attends upon him. A gentleman once giving a large party, just before dinner, went into his dining-room where the table was laid out, and observed a kitmutgar very handsomely dressed altering the arrangement of the table. The gentleman supposing this man was the servant of one of his guests, took no notice and rejoined his party. Great, however, was his surprise, when in a few moments his servants rushed in and informed him that he had not a single silver article left on his table. The smart kitmutgar whom he had observed, now turned out to be a thief, who had introduced himself to the servants of the house as the attendant of one of the gentlemen who had arrived, and of course was allowed to go in and out at his pleasure. He had been busied when seen by the gentleman in picking out the silver articles from those which were plated. The whole of the former description were carried off, while the latter were left untouched. The clever knave owed his success, of course, to his cool assurance, in taking no notice of the master of the house, or discontinuing his employment when he unexpectedly made his appearance.

We found Ghazeepore very unhealthy during the rains, and the bungalows being principally built of unburnt bricks were exceedingly uncomfortable. Some part of them used to fall down after every heavy shower, and the roofs allowed the water to come through in streams. While here I witnessed for the first time, what has been generally considered in England a traveller's tale. I mean a shower of fish. During the first rainy season we were at this station, I more than once picked up fish of three and four inches long in my compound,* and on the roof of my house after a heavy shower.

There are a great number of mango trees about this station, and the fruit was very plentiful. I also obtained some of the best pineapples while here that I ever tasted in India.

The Hindostanee name of the pine-apple is Onanas, and a very good story is told of a joke made by a young cadet in Calcutta on an old civilian with whom he was dining. The old gentleman was very prosy, and seemed inflated with pro-

* A piece of ground generally enclosed by a wall in the centre of which the house stands.

digious ideas of his own consequence. He told interminable stories about himself and his wealth, until every body got quite sick of them. At last, the young man could stand it no longer, and pointing to a pine-apple on the table, addressed his host as follows:—" Pray, sir, why is your coat like that fruit?" The leaden-headed elder considered for some time, but was unable to solve the riddle. " Because, sir," was the answer, " it is *on an ass*." (Onanas.)

During the rainy season we were much annoyed by the number of snakes and rats which infested our bungalows. These vermin absolutely swarmed in every apartment. The snakes were of the most poisonous description and of course exceedingly dangerous. I killed several in my bedroom, and my wife* was much alarmed two or three times by the appearance of a large cobra di capello, in her bath room. The venomous reptile used to come in through the drain which was made for carrying off the water, and she therefore desired the ayah† to stop the aperture up. This was done; but a day or

* It may little interest the reader, but as it is necessary to the understanding of some passages in the succeeding pages of this work, I may state that I married just before leaving Dinapore.

† A native female attendant.

two afterwards on going to take the customary morning bath, she was much frightened by the appearance of the snake standing erect, with his hood extended, in a corner of the room. On hearing her scream, I rushed to the place and soon with a stick despatched the intruder.

The opening of the drain, it appeared, had been partially stopped up by small pieces of brick; but the reptile had still managed to squeeze himself through. When inside, he had caught and swallowed a musk-rat, which so considerably increased his bulk, that he could not make his retreat by the small hole through which he had entered, and thus lost his life through his gluttony.

It is seldom that an European is bitten, although instances of very narrow escapes are constantly occurring. An officer of ours, one morning, put his foot out of bed into one of his slippers. The other fortunately was a little out of his reach, for on his getting up to take it, he discovered a small karait, a most poisonous snake, coiled up inside it. Had the slipper been near enough to the bed to allow him to put his foot in without rising, he would assuredly have been bitten and lost his life.

I remember, also, having had a narrow escape one night, in the rainy season, from one of the same species. It was so oppressively hot that I could not sleep. I got up and began to walk about the room, in which darkness was just rendered visible, by the dim light of a cheerag* burning in an adjoining apartment. While doing so, I remarked, what I thought was a piece of shoe-string lying on the ground, and put forward my bare foot to ascertain by the feel if I was right in my conjecture. To my astonishment it moved, and glided rapidly away. In the obscurity which veiled every part of the room, excepting where a faint gleam of the cheerag was thrown through the doorway, I could not perceive where it had retired. The next day, however, I had a regular clear out, and killed the gentleman in his hiding place under the mat on the floor. Such instances as these take place every day in the rainy season in India.

The musk-rats which infest the Indian bungalows are a great nuisance from the disgusting smell which they emit. So strong is this abominable scent, that incredible as it may appear, if a musk-rat runs over bottles containing wine or any other liquor, although they may be tightly corked and sealed, and the bottles covered with straw, the contents will be utterly spoilt, being com-

---

* A Hindostanee lamp made of burnt mud.

pletely impregnated with the vile odour of the vermin.

The common rats are nearly as great a plague. During the whole night they will scuttle and scramble about the house disturbing every body by their gambols. Their depredations, also, are most daring and quite in the wholesale line. I remember once at Ghazeepore, after a review, taking off my coat and accoutrements and throwing them down on a sofa. From among the things a silk handkerchief and my dress sash were speedily missing. As the natives are very fond of silk articles, I naturally suspected that the servants had stolen them, and, accordingly, they were apprised that if the missing things were not found their wages would be stopped to replace them. Some days after this occurrence, I discovered a rat hole through the false screen in front of the fire-place, and on removing it, not only found the missing handkerchief and sash, but about half-a-dozen napkins and towels which had been lost from time to time. These were all evidently carried thither and made into a bed by the rats. They must have taken the towels from off a wooden horse in my dressing room, and dragged them across two other apartments to their hiding place.

Mosquitoes and white ants also swarmed at

Ghazeepore, and we were not sorry, after having been at the station for two years, when one fine morning the route came with an order for us to proceed to Agra to relieve the 9th regiment at that station. The distance between these two stations is about six weeks' march. A great part of this was through a very good sporting country. Pea-fowl, partridges, quails and hares, were plentiful enough, and the jheels we passed literally swarmed with wild fowl. Shooting parties were formed every day after completing the usual march, and whole hecatombs of game fell before our Mantons and Purdeys.

The city of Agra is, I believe, one of the most ancient and extensive in India. There is a large fort on a most magnificent scale which was erected, it is said, by Akbar the Great. The interior of the palace and mosques is built of white marble, most beautifully inlaid with jasper, lapis lazuli and other precious stones; while the zenanas or women's apartments are most elaborately decorated with carved work inside and out. The casements which are composed of trellis work, cut out of slabs of marble, are unfortunately perforated in many places by cannon shot. The large black marble slab on which the kings of India were crowned is in this fort. The stronghold itself, the walls of which are very high, and of solid masonry, would

## THE TAJ MAHAL.          111

be impregnable to the force of any native power. There is a broad ditch which can be filled at pleasure from the river, and the outworks are numerous and extensive. It fell, however, to Lord Lake in the year 1800. Inside the fort may be seen the tombs of those officers who were killed during the siege.

But the greatest ornaments of which Agra can boast is the beautiful Taj, the eighth wonder of the world. This extraordinary building was erected by Shah Jehan as a monument over his favourite Sultana Noormahal. If his love alone inspired the conception of so magnificent a design, it must have been great indeed. It is totally impossible to describe the exquisite taste and workmanship displayed in this nonpareil of buildings. It stands on the side of the river Jumna in the centre of the most beautiful pleasure grounds, which forcibly bring to mind the description in the Arabian Nights of the superb gardens of the Caliph Haroun Alraschid. The tomb itself is raised on a large platform of the purest white marble. At each corner of this is a lofty minaret of the same material. In the centre is the Taj itself; which is also of white marble and surmounted by a dome. Round all the entrances are inlaid verses from the Koran, the letters being of black marble. The whole structure, inside and out, is most exquisitely carved, and covered with mosaic work, consisting of fruit and flowers of various coloured precious stones, so beautifully executed that they resemble the most admirable paintings. There are several apartments, and altogether the edifice is of vast extent.

It is said that Shah Jehan contemplated building another cemetery of like grandeur for himself, on the opposite side of the river, but death prevented his executing the design. The magnificent monarch was buried at the side of his beloved and beautiful bride in the lower apartment of the Taj. Their tombs are in perfect preservation, and are inlaid in the same manner as the inside of the Mausoleum itself. It has been built, I believe, about three hundred and eighty years; but from the state it is in, no one would imagine it could have been erected half the time. When I was first amid these scenes of enchantment, I almost expected to behold the vizier Grafar Mesrour, or the great caliph himself, popping out upon me from some of the mazy walks of the pleasure grounds.

The natives have a great regard for the memory of the " good Sultana Noormahal," who they say was as virtuous as she was beautiful. She gave large sums away in charity, and when she died, the people are said to have mourned as one man for the lovely being who ruled over them with so gentle and benevolent a sway. It is touching to behold the memorials of fallen greatness, and hear the legends of the warlike people who have now passed away, and are almost forgotten. Even the great capital of the Mogul dynasty,—in the hands of foreign adventurers, whose far distant island home is but a speck on the map compared with the vast dominions which their swords have won them in the East.

The whole face of the country, for many miles around the city of Agra, is covered with ruins and other vestiges of the powerful nation, which formerly conquered and held such extensive sway in India. Wolves are now the only inhabitants of the deserted palaces of the once lordly Moguls. They have taken up their abode in numbers among the ruins, and frequently at night prowl about the cantonment. Native children are often carried away by these grim visitors. Several instances of this kind occurred while we were stationed at Agra. A reward of ten rupees is given to any person who brings in a wolf's head to the magistrate. Half of this bounty is, I believe, paid by government on account of the many depredations committed among the juvenile population by these animals, and the other half from a fund established by the voluntary contributions of benevolent individuals.

The year before we were at Agra there had been a great famine throughout the North Western Provinces. Thousands of the natives died of starvation, and whole villages were depopulated. Many of these poor wretches wandered about the country, and, being unable to obtain food, offered their children for sale to any person who would buy them. The price they usually asked for a boy or girl of about four years old was five or six shillings. I have, however, known them to be offered as low as two for a rupee.* Large subscriptions were raised among the European residents of Upper India for the purpose of giving food to the famished natives. Hundreds of children whose parents had been starved were, by these means, rescued from the same fate, and comfortably clothed and fed. There was a large depôt for these unfortunates at Agra.

When first we arrived at this station, every one told us there was no shooting in the neighbourhood. We found, however, on trial that there was excellent sport to be had. Agra is, in my opinion, one of the best stations in India. It is extremely oppressive during the prevalence of

* One rupee, two shillings.

the hot winds, but less unhealthy than any other station at which I have been. The cantonments are extensive, there being barracks for one European regiment, and three Sepoy regiments, besides artillery. Agra was also the seat of government for the North Western Provinces. The deputy governor, Mr. R—, was universally liked by all the residents, and, I believe, he was very much regretted when he left the station, in consequence of that situation being abolished.

Great numbers of antelopes are to be found in the large meidans about Agra. These beautiful animals are, however, very shy and difficult of access. The best plan that can be adopted to approach them is by means of a stalking horse. In this manner I was frequently successful in getting within rifle shot. Their venison, however, is not very good, being dry, and generally destitute of fat. Among the ravines, which are very numerous about the station, is found a most beautiful small species of antelope, known by the name of the ravine deer. It is most elegantly and delicately formed, and differs in one respect from any other species of deer I have ever shot, both sexes being horned. The horns are small, smooth and sharp, and perfectly black. The colour of the animal itself is red, of nearly the same shade as the common antelope. They bound along over the broken ground at a great rate, and I used to think it almost a pity to shoot such graceful-looking animals. Speaking of the numberless ravines about Agra, a young cadet once observed, "he had never seen such a *ravenous* country in his life."

If the sportsman from Agra go down the river about ten miles, he will find on each side a very dense grass jungle. The ravines about there are all full of thick grass, in some places fully twelve feet high, and if he beats up these, he will assuredly have good sport at pigs, deer, black and gray partridge, quails and hares. Up the river there is also capital sport to be had, but as it winds much, a great saving in distance is obtained by proceeding to the best spots by land. At Koila Ghaut, about six miles from Agra, I have had good sport; and still better at Sameea Ghaut, which is about three miles farther; at Ghow Ghaut, about seventeen miles from cantonments, my friend P— and myself, killed nearly fifty brace of partridges and quails in a day, besides a number of hares. We rode out and home, and killed these birds after the usual morning's parade, and this was not till the ground had been thoroughly beaten by four other parties who had preceded us.

Wild peacocks are very numerous about Agra. I have killed as many as fifteen brace in a day, besides other game. The chicks when about half

## SHOOTING AT AGRA.

grown are most delicious eating, much better, in my opinion, than the floriken which is esteemed the king of game in India. Though certainly a delicious bird, its rarity, perhaps, is its greatest recommendation. The bastard floriken or leek, is sometimes found about Agra in the rainy season, but not very frequently. The young pea-fowl when rising out of the jungle six or seven together, put me very much in mind of the pheasant shooting in preserves at home. The old pea-fowl are generally very dry and tough, but they make capital mulligatawney soup which, I think, is the only thing they are fit for. There is no wild-fowl shooting at Agra, an occasional shot may be had at a goose or duck on the river, but nothing worth naming. The lover of rifle shooting may amuse himself by firing at the alligators, which are very numerous in all parts of the Jumna. During the day, numbers of these may be seen basking on the sand-banks with which the river abounds. Some of them are of great size.

The Mussulmans in India are very fond of game, but they are prohibited by their religion from eating the flesh of any animal that has been killed otherwise than by having its throat cut in a peculiar manner by themselves. I used to be in the habit of giving the greater part of the game, when I was out shooting, to the servants who accompanied me, and was often greatly amused by the eagerness with which they ran with a knife in their hands to every bird or animal which I knocked over. I frequently remarked, however, that when the animal was actually dead from the shot, they would still cut the throat, and vote, *nem. con.* that it was alive when they performed the operation.

The Rajah of Bhurtpore gave an entertainment to the European residents of Agra, while we were there. He had some large tents pitched near the fort, handsomely carpeted, and hung with a most singular collection of handsome glass lustres, gilt chandeliers, tin candlesticks, valuable paintings, and twopenny prints, mixed together in most heterogeneous confusion. He evidently thought them all very fine and well-matched.

We sat down in number about two hundred to a dinner in the European style, which was really exceedingly well got up, excepting that there was the same mixture of the best and commonest description of articles, as was exhibited in the adornment of the tents. Some of the plates and dishes were of the richest china, while others were of the meanest blue crockery, and handsome ivory mounted table cutlery was mixed up with the vilest black-handled imitations of knives and forks I ever saw. In the centre of the table was

## NAUTCH GIRLS.

an immense pie, to ascertain the contents of which much curiosity prevailed. At last it was cut open by some one near, when out flew about twenty little birds which had been concealed under this mountain of paste. The rajah seemed much tickled at the surprise depicted in the countenances of those around, and laughed till his fat sides shook again. It was, however, no effort of the obese potentate's own invention, hardly any native entertainment ever taking place without some dish of the kind. There was plenty of wine of all sorts, champagne corks were flying in every direction, and altogether the banquet was on the most liberal scale.

After sitting about an hour after dinner, the company were invited under a large canopy which was erected outside, and under which several troops of nautch girls were assembled.

These are generally in sets of three dancers, accompanied by a man who plays on a sort of fiddle, and another with the tom-tom. On commencing the entertainment, the nautch girls form themselves in a line, at some distance off, facing the founder of the feast, the musicians standing behind them. When the music commences, they all begin to sing and scream out their songs with a great deal more noise than melody. Keeping up their caterwauling, they advance and retire by a sort of shuffling step, twisting their hands about so as to keep time with the music, and sometimes covering their faces with their veils, and ever and anon throwing them open again. I believe the one who screams loudest is accounted the best singer by the natives, who are passionately fond of the nautch, while to Europeans it is insufferably tiresome. When one set have gone on in this way for about a quarter of an hour, and screamed themselves out of breath, they are relieved by fresh hands in better wind, who again enact the same game with little variety of entertainment.

The nautch girls are generally splendidly dressed, in bright coloured satins, and gauzes, and are profusely ornamented with gold and precious stones. Some of them have small golden bells attached to their ancles and toes.

After about two hours of this *nautching*, the company were informed that a variety of fireworks, which had been prepared for their amusement, were about to be let off. Most native entertainments end in a display of this kind, and the natives excel in pyrotechny. We all went into the meidan to witness this exhibition which was well worth seeing, although decidedly much inferior to what I have seen when a boy at Vauxhall Gardens.

## ICE ESTABLISHMENT.

At Agra, there was an establishment for collecting a stock of ice in the cold weather, sufficient to last for the three hottest months succeeding it. The means by which it was obtained were rather singular. A number of square pits were dug about three feet deep: these were nearly filled with a thick layer of straw, and upon this were placed a number of small flat earthern saucers. Into each of these was poured a little water every night, and in the morning, before break of day, there was generally a thin sheet of ice formed in each saucer. This was collected by a number of coolies* employed for the purpose, and placed in the ice-house, which was a pit excavated to some depth below the surface with a mud wall raised round the mouth, and thatched over.

The coolies lived in villages adjoining, and were assembled every morning by the beat of a large drum at the ice-house. This infernal drum used to wake me every day in the cold weather, about two hours before the bugle was sounded for morning parade; and, much as I liked the ice, I certainly often wished the drum somewhere else. The expense of making the ice was defrayed by a subscription, each contributor to which

* Native labourers.

sent his servant every night in the hot weather for a certain quantity. This, when delivered, was closely enveloped by the cooly in a couple of thick blankets, and immediately on arriving at home with his load, it was popped into a basket thickly padded all over with wool and closely covered. By this means the ice was prevented from melting for eight or nine hours, and any bottles of water, beer, or wine shut up with it were delightfully cooled.

No one who has not been in the East can imagine how great a luxury it is, in so hot a climate, to be able to get a glass of cool water. For six months in the year, it cannot be obtained otherwise than in a tepid state, unless cooled by artificial means.

## CHAPTER VI.

Rumours of war—Departure from Agra—Arrival at Meerut—March towards Affghanistan—Women of the 44th—The Begum Sumroo—Manufacture of shawls at Loodianah—Camels—Cross the Sutledge—The Punjab—Loss of baggage—The irregular horse—Forced marches—The Seiks—Crossing rivers—Cheyt Sing—Burial of the dead, &c.

ABOUT this period we used to hear rumours, from time to time, that things were not going on in Affghanistan quite as well as could be wished. At the latter end of 1841 accounts were received that the inhabitants had risen *en masse*, and beaten our troops on more than one occasion. An order suddenly arrived in January 1842 for the regiment to proceed to Meerut, which was hailed by every one as a prelude to a march upon Cabul. On arrival at Meerut, however, we were ordered to dismiss our baggage animals and go into barracks. In a day or two, one hundred men and three subalterns of the corps under the command of

Captain B— were ordered to proceed forthwith to the fort of Saharunpore as a guard over Dost Mahomed, the ex-King of Cabul, who was confined there. This was not likely to be a very pleasant duty, as the strictest vigilance was required, and we were given to understand that one subaltern would always be on duty, day and night, to keep an eye on the Dost's motions.

I was one of those named for this service; and four or five days after our arrival at Meerut, our detachment proceeded on the march to Saharunpore. On the march I found that an assistant surgeon of the Company's service, who had been appointed to take the medical charge of the detachment, was an old school-fellow. We agreed that after we had reached our encampment, and breakfasted, we would go out shooting, and have a talk of old times, should we find no game. Accordingly we did so, and had wandered five or six miles from the camp when we were overtaken by a messenger, who had been sent after us with the intelligence that an express had arrived in camp,

"Bloody with spurring, fiery red with haste,"

bringing orders for us instantly to return, and that the men were striking the tents, and getting ready for the retrograde march, as quickly as possible. We

## ORDERS FOR SERVICE.

lost no time, of course, in retracing our steps, and on our arrival in camp found the men just formed in the road, waiting for the word to move forward. Fifty voices together gave us the welcome intelligence that we were required on immediate service, and that Affghanistan was our destination. Orders had arrived at Meerut for carriage to be collected for the regiment with as little delay as possible. The women and children, and those men who were unfit for a long march, together with the heavy baggage, were also directed to be left behind, and the depôt to be formed at Meerut.

The route gave us Kurnaul as our destination: but we could form a very good idea, from the fact that the women were to be left behind, that we should not halt there. Such a bustle perhaps was never seen at Meerut before. The officers had just got settled in their bungalows when the orders arrived, and at every turn we met men hurrying about in search of pony trunks, as we understood tatoos* or mules were the only carriage animals to be depended upon in the rocky passes which we should have to traverse. I cannot conceive why we had been ordered, on first arriving at the station, to dismiss the camels and hackeries which had brought our baggage from Agra. About

* Poneys.

twenty days were wasted before sufficient carriage could be again obtained to enable us to proceed. This, too, was at a time when not a minute ought to have been lost, accounts having been received of the complete destruction of General Elphinstone's army, while it was further reported that General Sale was hard pressed at Jellalabad by Akbar Khan.

Our men were in the highest spirits, although the lamentations of their spouses were loud enough. We had heard of the appeal made by the widows of the 44th to the regiments ordered to Affghanistan. They called on them to revenge their slaughtered husbands, and every heart responded to the call.

As soon as sufficient carriage was obtained for the necessary baggage which was reduced as much as possible, we proceeded on our march. When we started from Meerut, instead of the usual tune played on leaving a station, "The girl I left behind me," the band struck up "The British grenadiers" and three hearty cheers burst from the men as soon as they recognized the national melody.

The first march was to Sirdhanha, at which place is the palace of the late Begum Sumroo. This extraordinary woman was originally, I believe, a Nautch girl, and was married by a French adventurer who had managed to carve out for himself a small independent sovereignty. She soon became tired of her husband, for whom notwithstanding she always affected great tenderness, and used rather singular means to remove him. She excited the troops to get up a sham mutiny, and surround the palace, clamouring for their arrears of pay. Her husband, who doated upon her, was induced by her apparent terror to order two palanquins to a back door, that they might escape from the infuriated soldiery. Before entering them, however, to quiet her apprehensions he swore that, should she lose her life, he would not survive her. By a preconcerted plan, his palanquin was allowed to precede that containing her to a considerable distance. Suddenly some of her attendants who were in her confidence overtook his palkee with loud lamentations, and showing a bloody handkerchief declared that the Begum had been murdered by the mutineers, and had sent him this token of her affection before breathing her last. Sumroo implicitly believed this story, and keeping his word, shot himself on the spot. On hearing the success of her stratagem, the Begum instantly returned to the palace, and distributing large sums of money to the troops wss by them hailed as their future sovereign.

Many stories are told of the Begum's cruelty.

One of her slave girls had by some means displeased her, when she ordered her to be buried alive instantly, and in her presence. When the living victim was immured in the grave, the Begum commanded her hookah to be brought, and smoked a chillum on the spot. Fearful even then, that her diabolical intention might be rendered abortive by some of her attendants not quite so hardened as herself, she caused her bed to be prepared, and absolutely slept upon the grave, to prevent the possibility of the poor girl's being rescued from her fearful end.

The Begum managed matters so well after her accession to the throne as to be guaranteed in the possession of it, during her life-time, by the English government. She was exceedingly hospitable, and used to entertain very handsomely any officers paying her a visit. She became a convert to the Roman Catholic religion, and built and endowed a very handsome chapel at Sirdhanha, after the design of St. Peter's at Rome. When we encamped near this place, I went to see this edifice, and met an Italian priest, a very intelligent person, who I imagine was the incumbent. He was very civil and communicative; and among other things shewed me where the remains of the Begum lay. A plain stone denoted the spot; but the priest informed me that a very elaborate tomb was being executed at Rome, and would shortly be sent out to mark her resting-place.

Our servants, who had been greatly alarmed at the disasters which had occurred in Affghanistan, even at this early period, put us to much inconvenience, by frequently deserting, and the strictest watch became necessary on our camel-drivers, who were equally alarmed, and sought every opportunity to make their escape, being fearful that they would be obliged to cross the Sutledge with us, which they looked upon as certain death. We arrived, however, at Kurnaul, without losing any great number of them. At this place, we received the route, directing us to proceed to Ferozepore which is on the extreme boundary of the Company's dominions. This march occupied us twenty days; and, had it not been for the trouble to which we were put by our unwilling attendants, we should have had a very pleasant march. The weather was not yet very hot, and there was capital shooting to be had near almost every encamping ground. We passed through Loodianah, where there is a large colony of Cashmerians, who manufacture quantities of shawls at this place. The prices they demand for them are enormous. I was much pleased at witnessing the manufacture of them, which is entirely by hand, and must be extremely tedious.

On our arrival at Ferozepore, we found a number of camels awaiting us, which had been collected by the commissariat officers for the transport of our baggage. Not more than half the requisite number, however, could be obtained, and of these many were not able to make a single march. We were obliged to pay the commissariat officer the whole amount of the money for the hire of those served out to us to Jellalabad, by which means we were deprived of any hold on their owners, who now had no reason to remain with us longer than they could avoid. Instead of every assistance being rendered us, going as we were on an arduous campaign, and to prevent the loss of our baggage by the desertion of these cameldrivers, their roguery was in every way encouraged. We had paid our money for the whole distance, and of course they made their escape as soon as they could. Numbers of officers lost all their property, in addition to the extravagant sum charged for hire by this absurd arrangement. Had the owners of the camels not been paid, until they had performed their part of the agreement, there would not have been one tenth of the inconvenience and loss which we afterwards experienced.

Having reduced our baggage as much as possible, to enable us to eke out the scanty supply of camels we had received, on the 10th of March

## CROSSING THE SUTLEDGE.

we crossed the Sutledge, accompanied by the 6th regiment of native infantry, some resallahs\* of Tait's irregular horse, and a company of foot artillery, the whole under the command of Colonel Bolton of H.M. 31st regiment. Ferozepore is thirty-six marches from Peshawur, through the Punjab, or the territory of the Seiks. The name is derived from two Persian words; *punj*, signifying *five*, and *ab* a *river*. These five rivers lay in our route; they are the Sutledge, the Chenab, the Ravee, the Jhelum, and the Attock, or Indus. Numbers of the servants deserted us here, and many officers were reduced to the necessity of tending their own horses and baggage animals. I had, however, been fortunate enough to retain all mine, excepting my grass-cutters and bheesty.† I was much inconvenienced for want of water by the desertion of the latter worthy, as the native servants will on no account do any work that does not strictly appertain to their own particular situations. The Sutledge is a muddy-looking river with numerous sand-banks, and has nothing particularly remarkable in its appearance. We crossed it by means of a bridge of boats, which had been constructed for our accommodation by the Seik government.

\* Troops.
† Water-carrier.

Shortly after arriving at our encampment, we heard from some of the followers who came in that an immense quantity of the baggage was still lying on the ground at Ferozepore, in consequence of the inability of a great number of the wretched beasts of burden which had been provided to rise with their loads. Some baggage, therefore, even at this early period, had to be destroyed. My camels came in late in the evening in a very wretched state, and I was obliged to throw a tent, and some other heavy articles, into the Sutledge in order to lighten their loads for the morrow.

The next morning we began to reap the fruits of the wise arrangements to which we had been obliged to succumb. About forty camels had deserted during the night, and the baggage of a large number of officers and privates was left on the ground, when the force moved off with no prospect of any means being obtained for its removal. Our commanding officer, who did every thing in his power to prevent the inconvenience to which we were put by those who ought to have known better, left a guard under an officer to prevent these things from being plundered, and to obtain some means of bringing them on. With great difficulty they did bring them in that night, after having been themselves the whole day without food or refreshment of any kind. This, on the first march from our own territory, was indeed an augury of what we had to expect further on. A guard was now ordered by Colonel Bolton to accompany the camels on the march by companies, and on their arrival in camp, after discharging their loads, another guard of troopers from the irregular horse was ordered to accompany them when they went out to forage. These men were strictly enjoined not to let them out of their sight until they returned to camp, when they where picketted within the line of sentries. In spite of all these precautions, however, numbers managed to make their escape every day, and, on leaving each encamping ground, officers and men might be seen setting fire to the necessaries which they had no means of transporting further.

The irregular horse who accompanied us were the wildest and most romantic looking subjects I ever beheld. They are principally the descendants of Pathan gentlemen, who, though reduced in circumstances, would not take service in the Company's army as ordinary troopers. In the irregular corps, they receive a certain monthly pay, I believe 25 rupees, for which sum they find their own horses, and arms, and consider themselves altogether different characters from the privates of the

Company's regular cavalry, as most undoubtedly they are. When they like their leader, they will fight admirably; and we had many opportunities of seeing those who were with us do their duty in capital style.

On our arrival at the Ravee, we were overtaken by Major Delafosses' troop of horse artillery, which had been sent on by forced marches to join us. This was another of the wise arrangements made by the authorities. We had passed through Loodianah where this very troop was stationed, and they received no orders to join us; but when we had nearly arrived at Ferozepore they were ordered to make double marches to overtake us. They effected the junction with the horses completely jaded by such extraordinary exertions. No wonder that when they arrived in Affghanistan the horses were not able to drag the guns. They had been knocked up at the commencement by unnecessary toil, and it was not likely that they could afterwards regain their condition with daily hard work, and but little food. We experienced much annoyance from the Seiks. These people were most hostilely inclined towards us, although their government was friendly. They are very fine looking men, but great boasters; and I have no doubt their cowardice, when brought to the trial, is as great as their bragging when danger is distant.

I have mentioned already that our servants were much alarmed by the accounts which they had heard of the prowess of the Affghans, and these Seiks made a point of frightening them still more. They told them that we were sure to be annihilated like the last force in Affghanistan, and that even if by some miracle we should escape, the Maharajah,* Shere Sing, had an army ready, in addition to which the Seik population intended to rise *en masse*, to cut off our retreat through their country. They were determined, they said, to exterminate the Feringees;† and our army was only now allowed to proceed in order that it might be more effectually got into the trap, with the Affghans in front and the Seiks the in rear.

These Seiks plundered our baggage on every opportunity. Our advanced guard one morning came suddenly upon a number of them while attempting to take some articles, belonging to the force, from the natives under whose charge they were, and had a skirmish with them. The irregular horsemen charged the vagabonds at once, and drawing their tulwars,‡ would have taken off a number of their heads in a very short time had they not

* King of the Punjab.
† English.
‡ Swords.

been stopped by the native officer in command. The robbers soon took to their heels, when they found what sort of customers they had to deal with.

General Pollock was at this time at, or near, Peshawur with a large force, and our commander spared no pains to overtake him. We had terribly hard work in crossing the rivers, none of which were at this time fordable. All our camels, artillery, and treasure tumbrils had to be transported in boats. The whole force, however, worked day and night to get them over with as little delay as possible. To induce the unwieldly camels to enter the boats was indeed no easy matter; but our men had heard that the Jellalabad garrison were reduced to the utmost straits, and they worked like men who knew not what fatigue was. The camel, I believe, is the only animal that cannot swim. It is an extraordinary fact, that the moment they lose their footing in a stream, they turn over, and can make no efforts to prevent themselves from being drowned. They have naturally a great antipathy to the water, which enhanced the difficulty with which we had to contend. Many became so much alarmed after they were in the boats that they jumped overboard and were lost.

A Seik envoy accompanied our force on the march. He had been sent by Shere Sing ostensibly to obtain for us any supplies we might happen to want, but really, I believe, as a spy. This worthy's name was Cheyt Sing, and a funny fellow he was. In person he was short and punchy, with a large good-natured looking face, and a roguish leer in his eye. He was very civil and obliging, and in consequence was asked to dine with us at the mess. He came attended by three strapping Seiks, as attendants, and although he informed us his religion would not permit him to eat with us, he would drink as much as we liked. Accordingly, he seated himself at a little distance from the table, and a bottle of port wine was delivered to one of his attendants. When Cheyt Sing was challenged to drink, another of his men pulled out a little silver cup which he filled and held to his master's lips. The old Seik was not long in emptying the contents; and, the moment he had done so, the third attendant stepped forward with a linen cloth and wiped his mouth for him. The operation was repeated whenever he drank. Every officer at mess made a point of challenging him; and, as he finished a bumper every time, he soon got royally drunk. He then began to be very facetious, and made many jokes in his own language which nobody understood but himself, his utterance, having become rather thick. However, they seemed to tickle his own fancy, for he laughed immoderately, and was eventually carried out by his attendants just as he had volunteered a Seik song, but of which, it appeared, he had forgotten both the tune and words. He dined with us several times afterwards, and said we were capital fellows; and condoled with us on our misfortune in not having been born Seiks.

Some of the inhabitants of the Punjab have an extraordinary custom of burying their dead with the head downwards in a small deep pit. The reason they give for it is this : they believe the world is flat, and that on the last day it will be turned topsy-turvy. The gates of Heaven they imagine will only be open for a short time, and it will be first come first served with the future inhabitants of the mansions of bliss. By burying their dead with the head downwards now, they will be standing on their feet when the world turns over, and thus according to their argument, they will of course be enabled to get into Heaven long before those, who being buried in the usual manner, will lose so much time in getting up from their recumbent position.

The Punjab, from the Sutledge to the Jhelum, is a most fertile and valuable district. I never in any other country saw such abundant crops of corn, and that the inhabitants are well off, there can be no doubt. None of that squalid misery was to be seen here which is so often witnessed among the native population in the Company's dominions. Even the common women employed in laborious work or herding cattle wore bangles,* and other jewels of pure gold and of great weight. In the Company's territory, the same class would decorate themselves with ornaments of pewter or brass. There is doubtless a great deal of money in the possession of the Seiks, and a campaign in their country would be a much more profitable concern than wasting so much blood and treasure as we have done in possessing ourselves of barren rocks and mountains. In Affghanistan, we gave rupees for stones; and our policy in ever going to such a place, renders us the ridicule of every native power in the East. No nation but England would take such a country as Affghanistan at a gift. The whole of its yearly revenue is about thirty thousand pounds, and our expenses there were nearly three millions.

It was said that it was necessary to take it, in order to prevent the Russians from invading our territories on that side. I do not see how we have furthered that object by converting a people who were inclined to be friendly towards us into

* Bracelets.

bitter enemies. Besides Russia never could send a power by that route. Supposing that the many hostile tribes inhabiting the passes and snow-capped hills, which they would have to traverse, could be purchased over by them, they could not obtain food for a large army, the country barely producing enough for its own population, and a small one would be useless. We could take possession of the Kyber pass at any time; and even granting that the Russians accomplished impossibilities, and traversed hundreds of miles of dreary wastes without food for themselves or forage for their cattle, they would ouly have proceeded so far to meet with certain destruction in the Kyber pass. Five thousand British troops, with a few guns, would defend that pass against an army as numerous as that of the Persian Xerxes; and the greater the number of the invaders, the more signal would be their destruction. Again, between the Indus and Jhelum is a succession of most formidable passes, which being held by British troops would be impregnable.

It must be a large army indeed of Russians to induce the British to take to the passes at all. Anything like a moderate force they would meet and overthrow in the plain at Peshawur, giving them every facility to arrive there for the purpose; and an army on a large scale, as I said before, would be defeated by its own numbers, the country being unable to furnish supplies to feed them.

We arrived at the Jhelum without the occurrence of any particular event. Here we were quite on classic ground, this being the river which Alexander the Great crossed previously to his night attack on the camp of Darius, who was encamped on the left bank. The ford by which he crossed is situated some distance above the town of Jhelum. At the season of the year at which we arrived, the stream is rendered very deep and rapid by the melting of the snow on the neighbouring mountains, and we were obliged to take everything across in boats. We had been delayed a great deal on our march by the wretched bullocks which dragged the treasure tumbrils and other stores; and Colonel Bolton, who was most anxious to be able to join General Pollock, before he should attempt the passage of the Kyber pass, at the mouth of which he lay encamped, determined to leave behind those clogs on our motions, to follow us in charge of an escort of some companies of the 6th native infantry, while we pushed on, by forced marches, in order to effect the junction as soon as possible.

From the Jhelum, the whole face of the country wore a changed appearance. Instead of fertile, well-cultivated fields, we now entered upon a barren, rugged succession of hills, which gave us a faint idea of what we should hereafter meet with in Affghanistan. Colonel Bolton discovered that a short cut of about twelve miles might be made by a path over the hills which would save us another day's march. The camels and baggage made a double march by the regular road, round the base of the hills, while the force proceeded by the mountain path. We had a regular climbing match; and our commander narrowly escaped losing his valuable Arab charger, which his syce was leading, it not being possible to ride. The animal once lost his footing, and was all but over the cliff. He struggled nobly to recover himself, and with the assistance of the man was fortunately successful.

The next two marches were through a strong pass, which would have been a teazer had it been defended by an enemy. On one of these marches, one of our officers seeing some wild ducks on a jheel, went round to get a shot. After he had fired, he was accosted by a Seik in a very insolent manner, who asked him how he dared to shoot the Maharajah's ducks; and, on an altercation ensuing, the fellow drew his tulwar* in a threaten-

* Native sword.

ing manner on P—, who had no other alternative than to present his gun at him. Some of the soldiers, however, saw what was going on, and running up, gave the fellow a tremendous thrashing. He was fain to ask pardon for his insolence before they let him go.

On arriving at Tameeak, despatches were received from General Pollock, who intended attempting the Kyber pass at once, ordering us to halt where we were, until the treasure and baggage which we had left behind at the Jhelum could come up with us. Accordingly, we were obliged to halt for four days at this place, where we were encamped on the side of a hill. There were some villages in the vicinity inhabited by a very fine race of people. Few men came into our camp who were under six feet in stature. They were very insolent, and more than once richly earned thrashings which they got from our men. One of our grenadiers, who was wandering about near the camp, observed a very clear stream of water, and being thirsty, went to drink some of the inviting liquid. A Seik who was near, seeing his intention, spat into the stream above him, and laughed in a scornful manner, evidently intending to insult him. The grenadier, however, soon made him change his tone, by knocking him down on the spot. The fellow screamed out, and above a dozen other men hearing him cry, rushed from an adjacent village with latees,* and attacked the soldier; but, being an athletic and determined fellow, he quickly knocked another down with his fist, and seizing his weapon, very shortly sent the others to the right about. Some of them had their heads badly broken, and came into camp to complain, but they had so richly deserved what they got, by the provocation which they gave, that no notice was taken of their complaint.

The country all the way from the Jhelum to Peshawur, is of the most barren description, and for military purposes excessively strong. Our road lay through passes formed by mountain streams, the bed of which, in many places, composed the only road; and the cliffs on either side are generally very precipitous. Over head hung large masses of rock, which seem to totter on the heights, from the edges of which they were suspended. By rolling down these masses of stone, the road itself might be easily blocked up, and they would furnish a formidable means of defence against an invading army. To crown the heights from below, would be excessively difficult. They are exceedingly steep, and generally do not lie in

* A long thick stick or club, generally of solid bamboo, and very heavy.

## THE MARCH.

continuous ridges, so that the ascents and descents for an attacking party would be interminable. The passes here are certainly nothing to the Koord Kabul, Jugdulluck, and some others; but before we had seen those frightful places they appeared very formidable, as no doubt they would be, if properly guarded. The others, if defended by Europeans with artillery, would be impregnable to any force under the sun.

The whole of this country formerly belonged to Affghanistan, and was conquered by the Seiks, who however were never able to penetrate a yard into the Kyber pass. They built a fort at Jumrood to secure their possessions from the incursions of the Affghans, who often sallied from that natural boundary of their kingdom, and gave the Seiks occasionally a great deal of trouble.

Our camel drivers still daily deserted when they went out, under the pretence of seeking for forage which was becoming extremely scarce, and it was impossible for the guards at all times to prevent their stealing away among the hills. To remedy this inconvenience as much as possible, the officers were obliged to buy food for their camels and not to allow them to go out to forage at all. This was forced upon them by the ridiculous arrangement to which I have already alluded.

When camels are hired in India, the owner has to feed them. In this instance, the owners said they were perfectly ready to do so, and would take them out to forage every day. The officers having now found out, by experience, that under that pretence they would run away with them, were obliged, rather than lose their baggage animals, to pay the extra expense of purchasing forage out of their own purses.

But, in spite of all our arrangements, they managed to make their escape, especially from the soldiers, who were not able to afford to buy forage, which was sold at an extravagant price. When about six marches from Peshawur, on turning out of my tent one morning to join the column, I found my camels were gone. They had been allowed to go out with the guard the preceding day, as the owner informed me that they were becoming ill by not being suffered to go to forage, in consequence of the food I was able to purchase for them not being so fresh as that which they could pick up themselves among the bushes on the hills. He assured me that he had no object in running away, as his home was in Peshawur, to which city he was going, and, pulling out a Koran from his bosom, he swore most solemnly and called upon the Holy Prophet to witness his oath, that he would not attempt to run away with his camels.

I was still unwilling to trust the man; but my servants persuaded me to do so, as the camels were not looking well. The fellow managed to slip away from the guard that day, and I was placed in a very pleasant situation when I got up next morning with all my baggage on the ground, no prospect of any means of carriage being obtainable, and the force just ready to move off.

I went at once to the commanding officer, who was always most considerate on these occasions. He immediately gave me leave to remain behind the troops, to see if I could not obtain some means of transport for my camp equipage and property. There were many in the same situation as myself, and I had just resigned all hope, and was about to give orders to set my tent and other things on fire, when I fell in with our quarter-master, who most kindly lent me two camels to take them on. I believe they were the only two spare camels in the whole force, and most fortunate did I esteem myself in being able to get them, it not being by any means a very pleasant prospect to begin a campaign without a tent or any clothes to my back, beyond what I stood in. A loss of the kind could not be replaced now we were so far from the Company's dominions.

When about three marches from the Indus,

## AN ANCIENT TOMB.

we were encamped near a very curious ancient building. It was in the shape of an enormous bee-hive, and the natives of that part of the country informed us that it was built by Alexander the Great, as a mausoleum over his war horse Bucephalus, which had died there. One of our subs, young P—, had himself let down by a rope from an aperture in the top of the building, and discovered below a marble slab on which was engraved a Greek inscription. He could not, however, decipher more than one word, which was, "ἵππος."* Many Greek and other coins were found here at different times, some of which I obtained, and have now in my possession. The natives of an adjoining village brought numbers into the camp for sale.

We crossed the Indus by means of a bridge of boats, constructed for our use by order of the Maharajah, Shere Sing. The river was at this time very high, and the current extremely rapid, which made it a matter of great difficulty to prevent the bridge from being carried away. The Seiks have a strong fort on the left bank of the river, which, being placed on the summit of an eminence, would completely command the passage of the river at any time. There are numberless

* A horse.

rocks in this part of the river which would render the navigation of it with boats extremely difficult and dangerous. We were much amused at seeing many of the natives floating down the stream on mussucks.*

They make long journeys in this way, resting their bodies on the inflated skin, and guiding themselves with their legs, which hang over into the water. In this manner they are able to avoid the danger of being dashed against the sharp rocks by the torrent; and seem to be carried down at about the rate of eight miles an hour.

The next day's march was through a very narrow and difficult pass, called the Geedur Gullee,† which name signifying that it is only a proper road for a jackall, expresses forcibly the opinion that the natives have of its difficult character.

We heard about this time that General Pollock had advanced, and been successful in forcing the Kyber pass; that he had proceeded on to Jellalabad in order to relieve General Sale, and that we were to follow him thither. The Kyberees had fought well, but the gallant 9th were not to be beaten back; they ascended the hills and drove the fellows off like chaff before the wind, in which

* The inflated hide of an animal, generally a calf.
† Jackall's lane.

they were ably seconded by the 26th native infantry and some others. Hundreds of Kyberees had been mowed down by the shrapnel shot from the artillery, and altogether they had sustained a severe defeat.

## CHAPTER VII.

Arrival at Peshawur—General Avitabili—Entertainments—Nautch girls—Hurree Singh—The Kyber pass—Ali Musjid—Scarcity of water—Heroism of a Sepoy—Brigadier Monteath—Skirmish with Kyberees—Jellalabad.

We arrived at Peshawur on the 21st of April, where it was necessary to halt for a few days in order to obtain some baggage animals to replace those which we had lost, and to make arrangements for the sick to be left behind. Our baggage was reduced to the smallest compass possible, in order that we might be impeded as little as need be in the narrow defiles through which we should have to fight our way.

Peshawur is a fine fortified city, and when we were there, was governed by an Italian general in the service of the Maharajah Shere Sing. His name was Avitabili, and he seemed just the sort of person to keep the turbulent and lawless population of Peshawur in order. At every corner of the city was erected a large treble gibbet, each of which had seventeen or eighteen malefactors hanging on it, as a gentle hint to the inhabitants to be on their best behaviour. I believe there was very little ceremony made with them. If a man looked sulky, he was strung up at once, in case he should be disaffected. Murder and robbery took place every day in the streets of the city, until the General used such energetic measures. Even when we were there it was not safe to leave the camp without being well armed. From all I heard, I imagine that Peshawur contains the most villanous population in India, and their governor, whose office it is to keep them in order, has no sinecure.

General Avitabili has a fine palace, and he kept open house to all the officers of the British Army. He gave splendid dinners, with abundance of wines and liqueurs of the finest quality, which were relished no little by us after the fatigues and privations we had undergone in the Punjab. After dinner, there were always twenty or thirty sets

## BATTLE OF NOWSHERA.

of Nautch girls in attendance, who danced pretty nearly the whole night. The old General seemed delighted with his guests, and did everything in his power to amuse them. I believe that all the expenses of the entertainments were defrayed by the Maharajah; but he could not have had a better deputy than we found in the jolly old General.

Many bloody battles have been fought near Peshawur between the Seiks and the Affghans: one in particular, at Nowshera, in which, after a long and doubtful conflict, the former were victorious, but with the loss of their gallant general, Hurree Singh. This brave leader had both his legs shattered by a cannon shot while the issue of the combat was yet uncertain. He refused to leave the field, and, being unable to sit on a horse, had himself placed on the back of an elephant from which he still continued to encourage his troops, and died just as their shouts of victory proclaimed that the day was won. The King was much affected when he heard of his death, and vowed he would rather have lost half his kingdom than his general. " The one," he said, " I might with his assistance have re-conquered, but I can never have another Hurree Singh."

I was fortunate enough to be able at this place to purchase two Cabul camels. These animals, although small, were far superior to those from Hindostan which accompanied us. Being born and bred in Affghanistan, they carried their loads without difficulty in narrow paths and over dizzy heights where the Hindostanee camels were continually losing their footing, and rolling down into the abysses below. It was another of their good qualities that they would not touch the foxglove (digitalis) which abounds in some parts of Affghanistan, and which the camels from Hindostan eat with the greatest avidity. This plant is a deadly poison to the camel, and we lost hundreds from its baneful effects.

After halting about five days at Peshawur, we proceeded a double march to Jumrood, which is about a mile from the mouth of the Kyber pass. This place was the most desolate looking spot I ever beheld. It was a large stony plain without a particle of vegetation of any kind, and bounded on all sides by bleak rugged hills which seemed to frown upon us in defiance. The pass itself is a very formidable looking place, and the day was spent by the soldiers in getting their arms well

FORT OF JUMROOD, IN THE VALLEY OF PESHAWUR.

Published by Henry Colburn, Great Marlborough Street, 1844.

cleaned, and fresh flinted, in readiness for the morrow, as it was expected we should be hotly opposed. Our force was very small to attempt a defile so long* and so strongly fortified by nature ; but the excellent arrangements made by Colonel Bolton would I doubt not have been successful had we been opposed by the whole force of the Kyberees.

At the mouth of the pass are two small hills. On each of these was placed a nine-pounder in order to sweep the sides of the mountains which command the entrance to the pass. The Grenadiers No 1, and the light companies of H.M. 31st Regiment, and three companies of the 6th native infantry formed the advanced guard under the command of the late lamented and talented Major Skinner of H.M. 31st. No. 1 ; and the light company of the 31st were thrown out as skirmishers along the heights on either side, followed by two companies of the 6th N.I. as supports. The hills were very high, and difficult of ascent; but by the persevering efforts of our gallant fellows they were effectually crowned in

* The Kyber pass is thirty five miles in length.

less time than could have been expected. The Grenadiers and a company of the 6th remained in the pass itself in order to clear the road and force any barricade which might be erected within the gorge.

The horse artillery followed, covered by Nos. 2 and 7 companies of H.M. 31st Regiment under the commanding officer, in person, and were succeeded by the baggage guarded by a part of the irregular horse; the remainder of the force constituted the rear-guard under the command of Colonel Eckford of the 6th N. I.

When we arrived at the entrance of the gorge, day was just breaking, but within the pass itself, from the shadow of the beetling precipices which overhung the narrow road, it was as dark as a wolf's mouth. To our astonishment we were not opposed, and we proceeded steadily and cautiously along the pass. The sepoys on the heights seemed in good spirits, and we could hear their shouts of " Ram, ram, Mahadeo,"* faintly echoed along the winding gorge from the vast heights above us. When broad day appeared we had a

* A salutation to the God Mahadeo.

FORT OF ALI MUSJID, IN THE KYBER PASS.

Published by Henry Colburn, Great Marlborough Street, 1844.

good view of the formidable defence which nature has created in this rocky inlet to the Affghan territory. The belt of mountains, a cleft through which is the pass, forms a complete natural bulwark against aggression on every side. We saw many mementos of Colonel Wild's disastrous attempt at forcing the pass. Dead camels and horses, broken and defaced military accoutrements, and human bones, lay scattered about in every direction.

After we had proceeded about three miles into the pass, the road was more open in some places; but again it became confined and difficult. We were a good deal delayed at times by the guns sticking fast among the large masses of stone, which choked the narrow path; but we at last arrived at Ali Musjid without accident or opposition. Ali Musjid is about eight miles within the pass, and is the first day's march. It is rather a severe one, the difficulty of the road making up for the shortness of the distance. The Musjid or Mahomedan temple, from which the place takes its name, is situated in the pass itself. On the peak of a high conical mountain, which rises suddenly here, is situated a fortress built of stone, which has been the scene of many a bloody encounter. The fastness itself is, from its situation, excessively strong; but it has the fault of many mountain strongholds: there is no water within the walls. A stream runs in the pass at the foot of the height; but the descent and ascent are both long and difficult, and on more occasions than one, when a slender garrison has been shut up here, they have not been able to get water, unless by stealth, and at night, to attempt which was rendered extremely perilous from the strict watch kept by the besieging Kyberees, and the deadly precision of their jezails.* A Mr. Mackeson, who was employed in surveying the pass for the British government, possessed himself of this fort by a *coup-de-main*, and with a few Affghans in British pay held it for a long time against the constant attacks of the Kyberees. The gallant Mackeson and his little garrison were reduced to great straits for the want of water, over which the besiegers kept the most vigilant watch, and they would inevitably have been obliged to surrender had not Mackeson's fertile imagination suggested

* Long rifle.

to him a plan, by which to obtain supplies from their savage enemies. The Kyberees and, indeed the Affghans in general, are remarkably tenacious about the possession of the bodies of their comrades who fall in battle. Whenever Mackeson repulsed an attack on his fort, he sallied out and secured the corpses of the assailants who had fallen. He used then to beat a parley, and sell the Kyberees their own dead at the rate of two mussucks* of water for each body. In this manner, he succeeded in supplying his little garrison until their food also failed them, when one night he quietly stole out of the fort, and succeeded in escaping with his men unperceived through the enemy, and arrived in safety at Peshawur. He was not a military officer; but in consequence of his gallantry displayed on this and other occasions, he was appointed to command the bildars†, in which capacity he afterwards accompanied us to Cabul.

Previously to Colonel Wild's unsuccessful attempt at forcing the Kyber pass, Colonel Mosely was sent forward with two native regiments to pos-

* Leather bags for holding water, each formed of an entire goat-skin.
† Native pioneers.

sess himself of this fort. The gallant Colonel made a sudden night march, and succeeded in his part of the enterprise without loss. When Colonel Wild however attempted to follow with the main body on a succeeding day, he was beaten back with a heavy list of killed and wounded with the loss also of his guns and great part of his stores and baggage. Colonel Mosely was now completely in a trap, for the Kyberees assembled in thousands to prevent his return, and he could receive no assistance from his defeated superior. Retreat however was inevitable, and to be effected at all hazards as the two days' provisions which his troops had been ordered to take with them were exhausted, and they were starving. Of this the Kyberees were aware, and they watched him closely. The retreat was commenced under a murderous fire from the deadly jezails of the Afredis,* who swarmed on every height commanding the pass. The loss was of course disastrous; but eventually the force effected its junction with the main body at Jumrood.

It was during this retreat that an instance of

* Name of a formidable and savage tribe which inhabit these mountains.

heroism was exhibited by a sepoy of the 64th regiment, which shows with what devotion the native soldier will follow a leader, whom he looks up to and loves, even to death. Shortly after leaving Ali Musjid, a young officer of the 64th regiment received a severe wound from a jezail ball which completely disabled him. He was accordingly placed in a dooly* in the rear of the regiment. By some means or other, in the confusion which reigned around, he was entirely separated from the troops, and the dooly bearers becoming frightened put him down on the ground and ran away. Unable to move, he was thus left to the mercy of their savage enemies, two of whom quickly discovered him, and, knife in hand, commenced descending the hill at the foot of which he lay. When they were within a short distance of the officer, he fortunately saw a sepoy passing by to whom he called. The moment this gallant fellow heard his voice and saw the danger of his officer, he rushed to the spot, and confronting the two Afredis, shot one, and bayonetted the other within a yard of their intended victim. He then turned to his superior, and expressed his regret

* A litter in which sick and wounded men are carried.

that he could not carry him out of the pass. "But, Sahib," said he, "although I cannot save you, I will stop with you; I have fourteen or fifteen cartridges left, and while these last, and I can use my bayonet, I will sell our lives as dearly as I can, and when I can fight no more we will die together." Saying this, he re-loaded his musket and sat down on a stone beside the officer.

Fortunately the officer's kitmutgar who had seen the state in which his master was left, fell in with his regiment. No sooner had the sepoys heard his account, than eight or ten of his own company stepped out of the ranks, and retracing their steps found him with his faithful guard. They then made a sort of rude litter with their firelocks and carried him in safety to the camp, which was eight miles distant. The gallant sepoy who so nobly saved him was immediately promoted to the rank of havildar;* and his conduct on this occasion will, it is to be hoped, be the means of obtaining for him still further promotion.

We had heard that we were to be joined at this place by a force sent to meet us from Jellalabad, under the command of our future brigadier. We

* Sergeant.

were appointed to the 4th brigade, under Colonel Monteath of the 35th native infantry. This officer's coolness in the hour of danger, and masterly management of the troops in action, soon gained the confidence of all ranks, while his urbanity and courteous demeanour to every individual won their hearts. He was beloved by the whole brigade. I hope he will live long to enjoy the reputation he has gained; and I am sure the sentiment will be re-echoed by every soldier who has served under him.

Brigadier Monteath had arrived, and was encamped within four miles of us, although we were not aware of his being so until the following day. Immediately on passing Ali Musjid, we arrived at a very narrow tungee or defile, about half a mile in length, with perpendicular cliffs on each side. It took us nearly the whole of the day to get our guns through this cleft; indeed, we were inclined to wonder, on looking back upon it, how we ever got through at all. It is fortunate that the summits of the cliffs which overhang this defile can be swept by the guns from the fort of Ali Musjid; for if only rocks were thrown down by the defenders posted on the top of them, every individual below must be crushed, and the road being stopped up in front and rear by the same method, it would be impossible to advance or to retreat. I was on the rear guard when we went through, and was jammed here for about six hours by the press of baggage-animals which could only effect a passage by single file. I often looked up at the threatening heights above us, and felt how utterly helpless we were. Six men from above could have annihilated the whole of us. Of course we should not have attempted such a place without previously taking possession of the heights, had they not been commanded by the fort which was garrisoned by our troops.

We effected our junction that day, and encamped at Lal beg Ghurree, about twelve miles from Ali Musjid. The pass became wider during the last eight miles of this march, and, although still very formidable, it was not so strong as the preceding part. We saw a great number of Kyberees congregated on the hills in the distance watching our motions, but they did not attempt to oppose us. Our brigadier had with him two companies of H.M. 13th regiment, a number of the 33rd N. I., and Backhouse's mountain train of artillery. These funny little guns, which are three-pounders, seemed almost like playthings. When about to be used, they are taken out of the carriage and each is put upon a mule. The carriage goes on another, and the wheels are conveyed by a third. It is astonishing what steep and craggy hills the sure-footed mules, thus burthened, will climb up. When arrived at the desired position, the carriages are put together, and the guns both mounted and fired in an incredibly short time.

We found about the valleys near Lal beg Ghurree numberless fields of standing corn which were a great prize, our cattle having had no forage for two days. No sooner had we arrived in camp than every servant and camp follower went off to the corn. Elephants, camels, tattoos,* and donkeys, were quickly loaded with the welcome grain, until they tottered under their loads; and for the two days that we were here they lived in clover. The camp followers, who had been on nearly as short commons as the cattle, had also fine feasting. They roasted the ears of half-ripe corn, and eat, and drank, and made merry. On

* Poneys.

the second day, however, the wells failed us, and we were obliged for want of water to change our quarters. The Kyberees had amused themselves by firing at the followers, who plundered their corn; but I believe few of them were hurt.

The next day we marched to Lundi Khanah. The pass during this march is really frightful, and I think it the worst part of the Kyber. The heights are terrific; but, as they generally lie in continuous ridges along the pass, when they are once ascended the road along the summit is comparatively easy. There is a great scarcity of water at this place, and no forage for the cattle. But the next day we proceeded to Lalpoora, and to our satisfaction bade adieu to the Kyber pass, having effected our passage without opposition, but suffering in many places very severe fatigue. At Lalpoora, we found forage for our cattle : and, as we were encamped on the bank of the Cabul river, there was no scarcity of water.

During the day, a rumour reached the camp that some Kyberees had carried off a number of the camels which were grazing on the hills. Some companies of native infantry were sent out to try and recover them, and a number of officers went out also. Pender and Tritton, of the 31st and myself, thought that we, too, might as well go and see the fun. Accordingly, we mounted our horses, and galloped away to the foot of the mountains. Not knowing which way the sepoys had gone, our only guide was the firing heard over the first range of hills. We determined, therefore, to leave our horses below, and, taking our double-barrelled guns, to cut across the hills in the direction of the reports, and try if we could not get a shot.

On the way we fell in with some sepoys and an old subadar* who joined us. I very narrowly escaped shooting a sepoy on this occasion; and, had it not been for the old native officer, most assuredly I should have done so. I was crossing over the summit of a hill, close under which the firing was pretty sharp, when I observed a fellow, whom I took to be a Kyberee, pointing his gun over a rock on the next hill at something below. I immediately presented my Manton, and was just pulling the trigger on him, when the subadar put his hand on my shoulder and exclaimed, " Sahib, sepahi hi." A sepoy it was, sure enough,

* Native commissioned officer.

who had come from camp in his native dress, which made me take him for a Kyberee.

The camels were eventually recovered, and five Kyberees shot. They were very large and powerful-looking men, and one of them made a desperate resistance. He got a ball in the leg, which stopped his running; and he then threw down his jezail, and drawing his long knife stood at bay. The first sepoy who came up to the spot he rushed at, making a desperate stab at him. Fortunately he missed his aim, the blade of the long knife passing under the Hindoo's arm. The blow, however, knocked the sepoy down, but he immediately jumped on his legs, and seemingly forgetting he had his musket in his hands, picked up a large stone and hurled it at the Kyberee, who was in his turn tumbled over by the blow. Jack Sepoy now seemed to recover his recollection, and stuck his bayonet immediately into the Affghan's body. To make sure work, I suppose, he fired his musket into him also. The muzzle being close to the man's body, the discharge blew a hole through him large enough to admit a man's arm, and set fire to his clothes.

The slain were soon decapitated, and the sepoys

carried their heads into camp in triumph stuck on the points of their bayonets. Among the Kyberees who fell was one woman who I believe was killed by accident. But she was fighting in company with the others, and a bag of bullets, I heard, was taken from her person. I asked a sepoy who was near, how it was that they killed women.

" Sahib !" said he, " she must have been killed by mistake ; but, as for males, I have lost twelve brethren in this cursed pass, and I would bayonet a Kyberee of a month old at his mother's breast."

Such a feeling among the soldiers was not to be wondered at. The Kyberees had mutilated and cut up those who had fallen into their hands in a most inhuman manner; and, although their cruelty in torturing their victims was avoided by the British troops, it was not likely that their lives would ever be spared when the tables were turned upon them. Throughout the war, however, mercy and protection were extended to the females by all.

The Nawaub of Lalpoora, by name Torabaz Khan, was always friendly to the British, and did them every service in his power. By his exertions the lives of Captain Ferris of the Jezailchees,* with his lady and sister were saved when the inhabitants of Pesh Bolak and Goulai rose upon his small force. The Jezailchees behaved splendidly, and succeeded in fighting their way to Lalpoora, from whence Torabaz Khan got them by a mountain pass over the Kyberee hills to Peshawur.

On leaving Lalpoora, we had to go through another pass which is called the Choota Kyber,† the passage of which we effected without opposition. Lalpoora is about eight days' march from Jellalabad, through a desolate, barren, country, and large stony plains, bounded by ranges of huge black mountains in the distance. We were much surprised that any race of people could be found to inhabit such a horrid country; but it is a singular circumstance, that the more barren and miserable a country may appear to others, so much the more is the *amor patriæ* strongly cherished in the bosoms of its inhabitants.

On arriving near Jellalabad we were met by

* Affghan riflemen in the British pay.
† Little Kyber.

numbers of the men of the 9th and 13th regiments who came out to see us march in. We could not help contrasting the clean and well-fed appearance of the late beleaguered garrison with the travel-soiled, half-starved looks of our own men. The officers of the 13th gave us a splendid breakfast on our arrival, and to which, it may be imagined, we did ample justice.

Jellalabad is one of the most miserable-looking places I ever beheld. It is situated in a large sandy plain, in which at that time there were not the slightest signs of vegetation. I believe that naturally the valley is very fertile, but having been so long the seat of war it had not been cultivated, and the cattle of Akbar's besieging army had eaten up every green thing, as effectually as if a flight of locusts had been domiciled there. The town itself is surrounded by a mud wall to which a parapet had been added by General Sale, and a ditch dug round the whole. These improvements, with the addition of some alterations at the posterns, and some small outworks, had materially strengthened the strong-hold. No means of defence, which could possibly be rendered available, had been neglected. All along the walls were piled heaps of large stones which had been collected and placed there, so that in case of an assault, the camp followers might, by hurling these missiles down on the heads of the assailants, be of material service in opposing their attack. A number of old Affghan pieces of brass artillery, which had been found when General Sale took possession of the place, were furbished up, and, being mounted on rude carriages, were so placed as to enfilade the ditch. One brass gun, the great Cazee as it was called, was mounted in a conspicuous situation on one of the bastions. This gun was about an eighteen pounder, and was very handsomely ornamented with various designs of fish, and most ungodly looking reptiles. There were also in the fort, I think, six nine pounders, belonging to Captain Abbot's company of artillery which had been furnished with Affghan horses. It was astonishing what difficult places these guns would go over without assistance from our men. It was by far the most efficient battery in Affghanistan.

The whole of General Pollock's army was now concentrated at Jellalabad. The cavalry consisted of H.M. 3rd light dragoons, the 1st and 10th

Company's light cavalry, and Tait's irregular horse. The infantry were H.M. 9th, 13th, and 31st regiments; the 6th, 26th, 33rd, 36th, 38th, 53rd, 60th and 64th regiments of native infantry and Delafosse's, Alexanders, and Abbot's horse artillery, one company of foot ditto, and Backhouse's mountain train. There were also Ferris's Jezailchees, Broadfoot's sappers, and Mackeson's bildars. I do not know the exact numbers of the force, but I suppose there were about ten thousand fighting men, and fifty thousand camp followers.

We arrived at Jellalabad and effected our junction on the 6th of May, and naturally looked forward to speedily continuing our march on Cabul. Great, however, was the disappointment among the officers, and loud the murmurings among the men, when at first days and then weeks passed away while we remained inactive. As the season advanced, the heat became intense; so much so, that it was impossible to live in our tents on the surface.

We were obliged to dig caves under ground to shelter ourselves, in some degree, from the burning heat. The camels and baggage animals were dying in numbers daily, and the stench of their dead bodies and of the filth of the immense camp was insupportable. Millions of flies were bred in the masses of corruption that lay on every side. The very air was black with them, and such torments they became, that it was almost impossible to get a moment's rest. Provisions were bad and scarce; and the price we had to pay for corn to keep our baggage animals alive, was enormous. Sickness began to rage among the men, who bitterly complained that they were brought there to die like cowards in that pest house, instead of being at once led against the enemy. Why this delay took place I could never make out: but, as we were subordinates, we had only to obey orders, and that without asking questions.

Sand-storms prevailed frequently in this abominable valley. For four and five days successively would they blow in our direction, and during this time we could scarcely see a yard for the clouds of sand which filled our eyes, our food, and in fact everything. It was, of course, impossible to keep it out of our tents, and, when we rose in the morning, our beds used to be covered an inch thick. To vary our delights, about twice a week we had

## MURDER OF A SOLDIER. 175

earthquakes, during which, the roofs of many of our subterranean dwellings fell in. An officer of the 3rd dragoons lost his life by an accident of this kind.

One night a man of No. 4 company of the 31st regiment was murdered by some Affghans who must have been prowling close to the camp. He was unarmed, and had just passed one of the sentries, when the latter heard a blow and a groan and instantly gave the alarm. It was a very dark night and the guard which turned out immediately were some time before they could discover anything. At last, however, they perceived the body of the unfortunate soldier lying in a ditch, not twenty yards from the sentry. He had evidently been attacked suddenly from behind, and his death must have been instantaneous. He had received a blow on the left shoulder from one of the heavy knives of the Affghans, which had nearly cut him down to the right hip. His backbone and ribs were completely severed by this single blow. He had in addition many cuts, I think eighteen in all, about the head, legs and arms. So quickly and quietly had it been done, that the nearest sentry had only heard the blows, and one faint groan. He heard no footsteps or scuffling, and was therefore unable to form a guess as to how many of the savage wretches had attacked the poor fellow; but there must have been several to give him so many wounds in so short a time.

There is a ferocity about the Affghans which they seem to imbibe with their mother's milk. One of the officers of the 9th regiment related to me an occurrence which took place during the action when they forced the Kyber pass. In storming one of the heights, a colour sergeant was killed, and from some cause or other his body was left where it fell. A soldier of the same corps happening to pass by the spot some time after, saw a Kyberee boy apparently about six years of age with a large knife, which his puny arm had scarcely sufficient strength to wield, engaged in an attempt to hack off the head of the dead sergeant. The young urchin was so completely absorbed in his savage task, that he heeded not the near approach of the soldier, who coolly took him up on his bayonet, and threw him over the cliff.

Various rumours and reports were at this time constantly floating about the camp. One day it was said that we were immediately to proceed to Cabul; on the next, perhaps, some story would gain credit that we were to return without striking a blow, and that the prisoners were to be obtained by negociation. Supplies of every kind had become very scarce; and a merchant who had ventured up with a small quantity of wines and liquors, sold them by auction at an extravagant rate. Wine, brandy and beer, fetched twenty shillings a bottle, sugar six shillings, and tea, thirty-two shillings a pound. The Jellalabad garrison had tasted nothing of this kind for upwards of a year. There was scarcely a bottle of wine or liquor in any mess in camp; while the water of the Cabul river which ran near was of the most deleterious quality. It was no wonder that the hospitals became crowded and numbers died of dysentery, brought on by drinking this polluted water, combined with the effects of bad food and tainted air. The stench of the camp was, indeed, enough to breed a pestilence, and much we rejoiced when the 4th brigade received orders to proceed to Pesh Bolak, and bring the Shinwarrees and some other hostile tribes to an account for their behaviour on divers occasions.

## CHAPTER VIII.

March to Pesh Bolak—Destruction of forts—Death of two officers—Their graves outraged—The Shinwarrees—Battle of Mazeena—Heroic conduct of four soldiers of H.M. 31st regiment—Return to Jellalabad—Sickness in camp—March towards Cabul—Remains of the 44th—Forcing the Jugdulluck pass—Dead bodies in the pass—Narrow escapes—Kuttasung—A take in for the Affghans—A forced march—Arrival at Tezeen.

PESH BOLAK is situated three marches from Jellalabad. We marched on the 17th of June, and arrived at Goulai on the 20th. Goulai is situated about three miles from Pesh Bolak. The people of that place were very penitent for their misconduct, and I believe gave a sum of money to be let off. The tribes about Goulai, however, had all absconded, leaving numberless forts and villages at our mercy. These we pulled down and utterly destroyed. Their wells, by means of which, they irrigated the land, were blown up with gunpowder and rendered useless. These people lived, in a great measure, on dried mulberries, as the land would not produce sufficient corn for their consumption. There were beautiful topes* of mulberry trees around the forts. Every morning and evening two companies from each regiment were sent out to cut them down.

We found out that by cutting rings through the bark into the heart of the tree, it was as effectually destroyed as if cut down; and it was a more expeditious plan as well as lighter work. It was, therefore, adopted after the first few days. We became quite adepts in the work of destruction, and a greater scene of devastation was perhaps never beheld. The Goulai people had, however, richly deserved it all. They behaved most treacherously and infamously to Captain Ferris and also to General Sale, and could, therefore, expect no better treatment when the game was again in our hands.

From Goulai we made short marches in various directions, levying contributions and destroying

* Woods.

the strongholds of those tribes who were refractory, while those who had behaved well, were rewarded and protected. We found plenty of forage for our cattle, and corn was to be had for the taking, so that in comparison to Jellalabad we were well off; and, as we continually shifted our encamping ground, we did not experience the same horrible stench and continual torment from the flies. Our cattle recovered their condition quickly. They had scarcely been able to stand under their loads when we left Jellalabad, but in the course of a fortnight they became quite fat. The heat, however, was dreadfully oppressive ; many men sank under it, and the effects of the pestiferous air of Jellalabad. One of our captains and one of the 33rd, N. I., died the same day, and were interred at a place called Katee. We buried them inside their tents, and picketed horses over their graves, in order that the Affghans might not be able to find out where the ground had been opened after we had gone, it being their constant custom to outrage the graves of their enemies. But in spite of our exertions to cover over the spots, we heard afterwards that they had discovered the graves, and having disinterred their ghastly tenants, had hung them up on two trees. The yellow jaundice became excessively prevalent among the troops, and I was unlucky enough to have a severe attack of it. I think this disease is one of the most disagreeable maladies a man can have. A continual nausea prevails, and it is weakening beyond description. It was a long time after I was convalescent before I recovered my strength.

Having punished all the refractory tribes except the Shinwarrees, who were always very hostile to us, we proceeded to Mazeena, which is about eight miles from their strongholds. This horde inhabited a very strong part of the country, and is one of the most independent and warlike tribes in Affghanistan. They had generally refused to pay tribute to their own sovereigns, and had sent several very insolent messages to us. General Monteath determined to see if he could not bring them to reason, and accordingly, the day after we arrived at Mazeena, a strong party of about five hundred men was sent out to reconnoitre their position under the command of Captain Willes of H.M. 31st regiment. They had not left the camp above a couple of hours, before the constant rattling of volleys of musketry announced to us in camp that they had been attacked, and were hard at it with the Shinwarrees. The reconnoitring party returned to camp towards the afternoon, when we heard they had had a very sharp skirmish, which had ended in the discomfiture of the Shinwarrees, but not without a heavy loss of casualties on our side.

They had effectually reconnoitred the Shinwarree valley, which was very narrow, with heights on either side, and strengthened by a long chain of forts. The hills were also covered with sungahs,* and altogether the enemy had a judiciously chosen, and very formidable, place of retreat.

Our brigadier now determined to attack them with the whole force of the brigade and make an example of them. Accordingly, the next day the force left the camp for the purpose, composed of H.M. 31st regiment, the 33rd and 53rd native infantry, part of the 1st light cavalry, Captain Abbot's troop of artillery and Captain Ferris's Jezailchees. The camp was reduced to as compact a size as possible, and two companies from each regiment with some cavalry were left to defend,

* Breastworks built of large stones, derived from the Persian word, Sung, a stone.

## BATTLE OF MAZEENA.

in case the Shinwarrees should make an attempt upon it. All the classies\* and bildars were provided with fire brands to burn the forts and villages, as soon as the enemy were dislodged from them by the troops. The Shinwarrees turned out manfully to oppose them, and a desperate conflict ensued.†

Our brave soldiers, however, were not to be refused. They drove the Affghans from rock to rock, and from hill to hill, with great slaughter, until they were completely beaten out of their valley, and took to the mountains. The whole of their forts, habitations and stores, were set fire to and destroyed. It was a complete victory, and the sepoys fought admirably. They were very fond of the men of the 31st, and were excited with a noble emulation of the gallant Europeans. The Jezailchees, as usual, distinguished themselves; and Captain Ferris, their commander, had two horses shot under him. Captain Abbot mowed down scores of the Shinwarrees with his shrapnel shells, which were

\* Tent pitchers.

† I was not personally engaged in this action, being at the time ill with the yellow jaundice.

thrown with the unerring aim for which that officer was always celebrated. A shot which he made, while besieged in Jellalabad with General Sale, is one of the most extraordinary on record.

About four hundred yards from the walls of the fort was a small hill, from which the Affghans used frequently to annoy the men on the walls of the fort with their long jezails. One day a party of them were making merry on the top of this eminence. In the midst of them was a piper; and they were amusing themselves by singing and dancing round him, and making gestures of derision to the garrison. Captain Abbot determined to try and spoil their sport, and accordingly had a mortar carefully loaded, with which, when he had taken his aim, he let fly. Whiz went the shell high into the air, and then descending, it struck the piper in the centre of the group upon the head, when it burst, and knocked over about twenty of the dancers. It is needless to add, that the Affghans never repeated their efforts on the light fantastic toe at that place again, which is called "Piper's hill" to this day.

Our loss in this day's fight was considerable; and the 31st Regiment had to lament the death of as brave a young officer as ever belted on a sword. He was shot through the heart in a most gallant attempt to take a sungah on the top of a hill at the point of the bayonet. Only five men were with him, and the sungah was defended by at least fifty Affghans. One of his men was severely wounded at the same moment. When poor McIlveen received the ball, he sat down on a stone and said to the four unwounded soldiers who remained:

"They are too strong for you now, men. They will come at you directly; you had better retreat. Do not encumber yourselves with my body; but take my sword, I should like that to be sent to my mother. I feel very weak."

With these words, he fell back and expired. The Affghans seeing the effect of their fire, rushed down with frightful yells, brandishing their knives, to cut up the bodies according to their invariable custom. But the four brave 31st men determined to die rather than leave their officer's body to be mutilated; and, forming in line before him, they let the enemy come within ten yards of them, when, by a well-directed fire, they killed four and wounded some others. The enemy, not expecting such a warm reception, were panic-struck, and ran back to their breast-work, when the brave fellows retreated, bearing with them the body of young McIlveen and their wounded comrade. The soldiers even brought home a door from one of the destroyed forts, and from the wood manufactured a coffin for their officer, so universally was the right feeling towards their superiors diffused among the men of the 31st.

Poor McIlveen fell in his first fight; but he died like a soldier, and was deeply regretted by every individual in the corps.

The Shinwarrees, in addition to the destruction of their strongholds and habitations, had experienced a very heavy loss in killed and wounded. Their chief, Sekunder Khan, was at this time absent in attendance on Akbar Khan, at Cabul; but his whole family had fallen in these two actions. The tribe was effectually humbled; and they sent deputies into our camp the succeeding day to beg for mercy, and offering to send in hostages to Jellalabad for their good behaviour. Crest-fallen as they were, Brigadier Monteath granted their petition; and orders having been received from General Pollock, to recall us to Jellalabad, from which place we had been absent six weeks while proceeding with our work of destruction, we commenced our retrograde march, and arrived at Jellalabad on the 3rd of August, much to the disgust of us all. We had smelt the camp for some miles before we arrived at it, and found sickness raging both among the men and the beasts of burthen. They were dying by hundreds; and we had no sooner taken possession of the holes in which we had burrowed previously to our little expedition, than our hospital again became crowded. I was still suffering from the effects of the severe malady with which I had been afflicted. In fact, it was impossible to regain health in the abominable pestilential camp at Jellalabad. All our men looked liked ghosts; and hundreds of brave fellows met their deaths ignobly here, whose hope it had been, when their last hour should come, to die like soldiers in the presence of an enemy.

To add to the miseries which I was suffering at this period, I received a packet of letters from England, acquainting me with the death of a beloved and most amiable sister, whose end, although for some time expected, I mourned most deeply and sincerely. A far severer trial, however, awaited me. Another letter came, and in it the intelligence that my kind and most indulgent father had been also taken away. He had died suddenly, two months after my poor sister and in the possession of the most vigorous health up to the moment of his decease. He was the best of parents : his sole thought was the happiness of his children, for whose welfare no sacrifice was too great. I had buoyed myself up through all the trials and perils which I had undergone, with the anticipation of delighting his fond heart with the recital of my adventures. The blessing which accompanied his farewell when I left home seven years before, still sounded in my ears ; and the news of his unexpected demise came upon me with withering effect. I had never thought of his death ; and that he should be laid in his last home, while I, thousands of miles away, could not even look on his cold remains was too much to bear. I was seized with a fever, which probably would have laid me up for some time; but fortunately, just at this time, the welcome intelligence arrived, that we were at last to break up the camp, where so many months had been wasted n inactivity, and proceed at once to rescue the prisoners in the hands of Akbar Khan, and to destroy Cabul, as a punishment for the treachery of the Affghans. I used my utmost efforts to shake off my illness, at the thought of at last meeting the enemy, and revenging our fellow comrades who had been so barbarously cut up in the snow.

I was still weak when we marched from Jellalabad on the 23rd of August; but, during a week's halt at Futtiabad, made for the purpose of collecting provisions, I quite recovered my health and spirits. At this place, Captain Marshall, another excellent officer of the 31st regiment, sank under the exposure and privations which he had undergone during the campaign. By his death a company became vacant, of which, to my delight, I was appointed by the commanding-officer to take charge and command. It was the company in which I had first begun my career as a soldier, and therefore the command of it in action was doubly acceptable.

From Futtiabad it was decided that the army

should proceed in two divisions. The second, under the command of General McCaskill, was very small in proportion to that commanded by General Pollock in person.

From Futtiabad we proceeded to Gundamuck, when the road again began to be very difficult, and was commanded by heights on every side. An entrenched camp was formed here, in which were left some native troops in order to keep the road partially open in our rear. A body of about four thousand Seiks, who had followed us to Jellalabad, were also left behind, with the exception of about five hundred who were to go on with us to Cabul, and who were appointed to join the 2nd division. Gundamuck was the last place at which we could hope to obtain forage of any kind for our cattle, the next eight marches being through a succession of most formidable passes, and over mountains on which not a blade of vegetation of any kind could be found: all was barren rock.

It was necessary to carry every ounce of food for eight days' consumption, for our baggage animals and the camp followers and sepoys were in the same predicament. It may be readily conceived what a train of baggage we had to protect, although every thing was reduced as much as possible. Eight days' food for sixty thousand men, and for about fourteen thousand baggage animals, besides that for the horses of the cavalry and artillery, must be carried, or the army would be starved on the road. When it is considered that, in many places one camel only could go at a time, the difficulty and delay in getting through these marches may be imagined. For hours and hours sometimes would the baggage animals be jammed together in some of the narrow gorges without progressing an inch on the way. A march here of ten miles, generally took us twelve or fourteen hours, and the rear guard was frequently near twenty-four hours in performing the distance.

The first division, which comprised four fifths of the whole strength of the army, marched from Gundamuck on the 6th of September. The second followed on the 7th; and in consequence of its numerical inferiority was subjected continually to the furious attacks of the savage tribes who defended the road, while the other, for the most part, from its formidable appearance overawed them.

Near Gundamuck, on the right of the road, is

the hill on which the remains of the unfortunate 44th made their last stand. The sepoys, who composed the principal force of General Elphinstone's army, had nearly all sunk under the hardships which they experienced, or were killed by the enemy long before arriving at this place. The wreck of the army, which consisted of about one hundred and seventy men, principally Europeans, being unable to proceed further, determined to come to bay here and sell their lives as dearly as they could. They had, I heard, but two cartridges among them, and with these two of the advancing enemy were sent to their last account. The others poured upon the exhausted and worn-out soldiers by thousands; and, after a bloody conflict, the enormous numerical superiority of the Affghans gave them the victory. Every one of this gallant remnant of the army was killed, except Captain Souter, and a drummer of the 44th. The gallant Captain Souter preserved his life by having saved the colours of his regiment. He had them wrapped round his body, and an Affghan chief taking him from his extraordinary trappings to be a person of great distinction, ordered his life to be spared, thinking probably to get hereafter a good ransom for his prisoner. On unwrapping the colours from his body afterwards, Captain Souter found they had twice saved him from death, two bullets having been lodged in the folds of the silk.

When opposite the hill, the column was impeded for some time, the guns having stuck fast; and, while the men were getting them to rights again, I ascended the eminence to see the remains of the gallant fellows who had fallen there. The hill was very steep, covered with large masses of stone, and difficult of ascent. Had they possessed ammunition, they might have made a stand for some time on it. The top of the hill was thickly strewed with the bodies of the slain. Some were mere skeletons, while others were in better preservation. Their hair was still on their heads, and their features were perfect, although discoloured. Their eyes had evidently been picked out by the birds of prey, which, wheeling in endless gyrations above my head, seemed to consider me an intruder on their domain. On turning the corner of a large rock, where five or six bodies were lying in a heap together, a vulture which had been banquetting on them hopped carelessly away to a little distance, lazily flapping his huge wings, but too indolent to fly. He was evidently gorged with his horrid meal; and, as the foul bird gazed listlessly at me, I almost fancied him the genius of destruction gloating over his prey. I turned from the sickening sight with a sad heart, but a stern determination to lend my best efforts towards paying the Affghans the debt of revenge we owed them.

We got to Soorkab, the first march from Gundamuck, at about three o'clock in the afternoon. The road in many places was extremely difficult, but we were not opposed. When we arrived at Soorkab, the rear guard of the first division had not moved from the encamping ground; we could see their enormous lines of baggage animals stuck fast in the narrow winding mountain path, which is the only road. The officers of the rearguard informed us that the train of baggage had not moved for eight hours. About a couple of hours after we arrived in camp they began to stir, and wound slowly from our sight. We saw many Affghans on the heights which towered thousands of feet above our heads, but they molested us no further than firing occasionally at our piquets during the night.

The next morning, shortly after day-break, the division moved off towards Jugdulluck. This was one of the most difficult marches which we experienced. General M'Caskill was too ill to sit on horseback: he proceeded, therefore, in a dooly,* while the command devolved on Brigadier Monteath. Jugdulluck is about fourteen miles from Soorkab. The first three miles of the road is over a range of hills by a winding and very narrow and rocky path. It then continues for about eight miles through a formidable pass, but not what is generally called *the pass*. This devil's cleft turns off to the left at almost a right angle with the road, and was the most terrific place I had then ever beheld. There is a steep descent into the mouth of it; and from the gloom and darkness in which the narrow and formidable gorge is veiled, it would require no great effort of the imagination to fancy it the regular road to the infernal regions. The Ghilzees attacked us in great force on the way, and kept up a sort of running fight during the whole march.

At the mouth of the " descensus averni," or *the*

* A kind of litter carried by four men.

*pass*, is a small *plateau* of level ground, to command which, sungahs had been erected by the enemy on some neighbouring hills. When we had arrived at this place, beating the Ghilzees before us, it was getting very late in the day, and we could make out by the continual heavy firing behind us, that our rear-guard was very hotly engaged with the enemy. As night was closing in, our gallant brigadier, with his usual penetration, foresaw that our little rear-guard would be placed in a very perilous situation, while the baggage animals were defiling through the pass, and would not from the smallness of its numbers be able to protect the long line of baggage from the attacks of the enemy. He, therefore, most judiciously halted the main body on this *plateau*, and ordered the baggage to be taken immediately through the pass after the advanced guard. I was sent with a sub-division to take possession of the sungah on the hill to the left of the road, and my subaltern with the like force to take that on the right. By these means, the rear-guard being largely reinforced at the mouth of the pass, could easily keep the enemy off, while the advanced guard protected the baggage into camp.

From the sungah of which I had taken possession, I could see our gallant little rear-guard, under the command of Colonel Bolton of the 31st Regiment, coming leisurely along the road in rear of the long line of camels, literally enveloped in fire and smoke. Clouds of Ghilzees were following it up, and the rattling of their jezails was incessant. Ever and anon a party of the soldiers would be sent out, and I could see them driving the enemy before them like sheep. They again, however, returned to the attack as soon as the pursuit was discontinued; and, although numbers of them were continually dropping under the well-directed fire of our men, still they came on like so many devils. Their ferocious yells might be heard above the din of the battle; and, had not the main body of our division been halted where it was, our brave fellows who composed the rear-guard would have been placed in a critical position, the enemy out-numbering them in the proportion of more than twenty to one. In about two hours, the whole of the baggage was got through, while we kept the enemy off by a constant fire on them from our position. The rear-guard, having effectually routed the Affghans with whom they had so long sustained the arduous and bloody contest which I have endeavoured to describe, effected its junction with us. They had suffered severely; and their gallant leader had his horse wounded in two places under him, but the enemy had received a severe lesson. Every obstacle which could impede the passage of the defile having now been overcome, we again formed in column of march; and, giving the Ghilzees a farewell volley, we entered the pass.

I shall never forget the sight I saw here. The poor fellows, who had fallen in Elphinstone's retreat, lay together in heaps. Their bodies absolutely choked up the narrow pass, and our men were marching in a pulp of human matter. It was impossible to avoid treading down the dead, who were lying in hundreds in the road; the caves on either side were also full. The bodies were in extraordinary preservation: the features of several of the slain being recognized as those of old friends by many of our officers and men. This pass is exceedingly narrow, in some places being not more than ten feet broad. As we were marching along about half-way through the pass, a volley was poured upon us by a number of Ghilzees, who had again collected on the heights, and several of our men dropped. A most furious action now commenced; but the Affghans having been disheartened by the loss which they had suffered, during the former part of this hotly-contested march, soon gave way, and molested us no more, except by a few occasional long shots.

When we were nearly out of the pass, I saw the flash of a jezail from a hole in the side of a hill, not thirty yards from us, and immediately one of our men dropped, shot through the body. I pointed the place out, and several of the men ran up, and fired their muskets into the hole. One of them then crept in, and dragged out the body of an Affghan, with four balls through him. This circumstance will give the reader an idea of the shifts these people make use of to harass an enemy. Often have I been in a heavy fire, without being able to see an enemy, who were undoubtedly hidden away in caves about the mountains, which are not easily distinguished, being generally covered by stunted holly bushes, the only kind of tree or shrub that grows on these barren hills.

An officer of ours, Lieutenant Shaw, had a very narrow escaape during this day's action. He was on the advanced guard with his company, a sergeant of which being severely wounded and obliged to walk, there being no means of carrying him, in order to lighten his load, Lieutenant Shaw took his musket from him. No sooner had Shaw put it on his shoulder, than a bullet struck the gold cord below it, and, slightly wounding the flesh, flattened on the lock-plate of the musket, the stock of which it broke. Had the musket not been there, the ball of course would have gone through his neck, and most probably killed him on the spot. A soldier almost immediately afterwards, while loading his musket, had the lock-plate struck by another ball, which, had not his weapon been in the priming position, would have gone through his hip. Numberless narrow escapes of this kind take place in every action, which would almost appear incredible. Captain Urmston of the 31st, at the battle of Mazeena, was saved from a severe wound from a bullet, which struck, and was flattened on his sword while hanging at his side.

The next morning the march was continued

## AN UNWELCOME RECEPTION.

towards Kuttasung. The enemy annoyed the column by firing from the heights, and another officer of the 31st Regiment and some men were wounded. Captain Baldwin of the 31st, with his company was on piquet here; and he managed, by concealing his men on one of the hills after the rear-guard had moved off the encamping ground, to get a fine shot at a party of Affghans who had come down to see what plunder they could lay hold of. They ascended the very hill over the brow of which B— lay *perdu*, and came on to within about thirty yards, when the soldiers sprang up and poured a volley into them, which dropped some thirteen or fourteen of the party. Such a scrambling was never seen before. The survivors probably thought, from the suddenness of the attack, that they had unwittingly come in contact with the main body of the British army. They took to their heels at once; and many in their haste, losing their footing on the steep descent, rolled headlong over each other to the bottom, the soldiers indulging in shouts of laughter at the panic, which the success of their trick had caused among the Affghans.

The enemy attempted nothing during this march beyond some attacks on the baggage, in which they were repulsed; but their constant firing on the column was exceedingly annoying. It is astonishing at what an enormous distance the fire from their long heavy rifles is effective. Our men were continually struck with the Affghan bullets, when we could reach the enemy with nothing under a six-pounder. Our muskets were useless when playing at long bowls. The fact is, our muskets are about as bad specimens of fire-arms as can be manufactured. The triggers are so stiff, that pulling them completely destroys any aim the soldier may take; and, when the machine does go off, the recoil is almost enough to knock a man backwards. Again, the ball is so much smaller than the bore of the barrel that accuracy in its flight, at any considerable distance is impossible. The clumsy flint locks, also, are constantly missing fire.

During this march, and the last, the road was covered with the bodies of dead camels and bullocks, which, being unable to proceed farther, had been shot, and their loads burnt by the preceding division, to prevent their falling into the hands of the enemy. We were obliged to destroy scores of the wretched beasts in the same way, and the stench of their rotting bodies was insupportable on our return.

During this march we passed the barricade which the Affghans had built across the road to intercept the retreat of the late unfortunate army. The men of the horse artillery having abandoned their guns, had acted as cavalry for some time before the arrival of the discomfited force at this place. They made a furious charge at the barricade, and were all killed in the attempt to force it. The Affghans said that the Feringhees had fought most desperately here, and allowed that their own loss in defending the barricade against their attacks had been very severe. Captain Dodgin of the 44th, an officer with only one leg, but a most determined and powerful man, had killed with his own hand five of the Affghans before he was overpowered. The bodies of the poor fellows and those of their horses were lying very thickly about. In a small ruinous fort on the left of the road they were in heaps. They were hacked about in a most frightful manner by the long knives of the savage Affghans, and, from the position and number of the slain, there had been evidently a most desperate conflict within the fort.

The enemy had of course removed their own slain; but Akbar Khan himself allowed, that five thousand of his men had fallen in the pursuit of the worn out and starved army of General Elphinstone, the greater part of whom having no ammunition, were reduced to the necessity of using the butt ends of their firelocks as the only means of defence. Fifteen thousand men had fallen between Cabul and Gundamuck; but not above five thousand of the number were fighting men, the remainder being composed of camp followers and sick and wounded European and native soldiers, who could not use their arms. The greater part of those perished in the snow about the passes of Koord Cabul and Tezeen. But one man of the whole army escaped, Dr. Brydon, who, although severely wounded, managed to get into Jellalabad, bearing the news of the disaster to the garrison.

At Kuttasung, I was on piquet with my company, and the enemy kept us on the alert by occasionally favouring us with a few shots. No damage, however, was done. When the rear-guard moved off in the morning, the piquets were ordered to retain their position on the heights until the guns were dragged up a steep eminence which presented itself on the commencement of the march, and which could be completely swept by an enemy occupying the position in which we were. While this delay took place, I had some good fun with a number of Affghans who had come down to our late encampment, and were trying to take possession of a half-starved and worn out bullock, which had been overlooked by the party whose duty it was to destroy all such baggage animals as were unable to proceed. The brute was just within gunshot of my piquet, and the Affghans who were dodging about the large stones of the valley, were saluted by a shot whenever they showed themselves, which they were obliged to do when running from behind one rock to another, coming nearer the coveted prize each time. Some three or four of them got the worst of this sort of fun, but at last one desperate fellow, stealing from behind a stone, seized the bullock's halter, and, although saluted with a volley of musketry, he was so active in dodging about from one place of cover to another, that he led it some distance away. A ball at last, however, struck the ground close by him, and he let the animal go, and ran off to a respectful distance, seemingly waiting until we should take our departure. When we were ordered to move off, in order to join the rear-guard, I have no doubt they had a fine fight among themselves for the prize.

The rear-guard was under the command of the late talented and distinguished Major Skinner of the 31st regiment. When we joined it, we heard that an express had been received from General Pollock, ordering us to make a forced march of the next two regular marches, and join him in the valley of Tezeen. This was the most fatiguing and difficult march that we experienced; the artillery horses were knocked up, and our men had to drag the guns nearly the whole way. The enemy annoyed us very much on the road, disputing the ground inch by inch, and making several attacks on the baggage, in all of which, however, they were repulsed with loss. We arrived in camp long after dark, completely knocked up, and not till we had been obliged to shoot one elephant, sixty-five camels, and fifty-five bullocks, and to destroy their loads, principally consisting of provisions for the army. The poor brutes had fallen down from exhaustion on the road.

I saw a horrible sight, while we were on this march. It was a heap of above fifteen hundred dead bodies of sepoys and camp followers who had belonged to the army of General Elphinstone. These poor wretches, we heard, being unable to retreat farther, had huddled themselves together in a group for the purpose of affording mutual warmth to their frost-bitten limbs. When the cruel enemy discovered them, they barbarously stripped the poor unfortunates of their scanty clothing, and left them naked in the snow to die of cold, reviling them with bitter taunts, and refusing to put them to death at once, although the poor wretches prayed them to do so as the greatest charity they could shew them. Many of these bodies were those of women and children.

We fired a few shells from a howitzer during the evening at a body of the enemy, who annoyed us considerably while we were dragging the guns up a hill, a short distance from the camp; and the sight of the shells spinning into the air, together with the glare of the lighted fuses had a most beautiful effect in the darkness which had succeeded the brightness of the day. When the shells burst, they quite illuminated the sides of the hills, and we could see by their light the enemy tumbling about on all sides when one luckily alighted among them.

## CHAPTER IX.

Valley of Tezeen—Night attack—Battle of Tezeen—Storming the left heights—A charge of bayonets—A fat chief—Arrival at Koord Cabul—Scene within the pass—Arrival at Cabul—Rescue of the prisoners—Noble conduct of Akbar Khan—Capture of Cabul—British Flag hoisted in the Bala Hissar—Artillery taken—Extraordinary recovery of a Will—Arrival of General Nott—Battle of Istaliff—Destruction of Cabul.

NOTHING was gained after all by this forced march. The cattle were so completely knocked up, that the whole army was obliged to halt the next day. Had we been allowed to perform the two marches in the regular manner, we should have effected our junction with the first division without one fifth the loss of stores, on the same day which we were thus obliged to waste by halting.

During this day, our piquets were constantly engaged with parties of the enemy on the hills; and in the afternoon the gallant Colonel Taylor of the 9th, took his regiment out, in order to recover the body of a sergeant of the corps, who had been killed in the morning, and left on a hill. It was a beautiful sight from below to see the brave 9th beating the fellows over the mountains. The enemy were in great force, and fought manfully; but were at last completely broken and dispersed, leaving many dead behind them. During the night, however, they made furious attacks on the piquets, and on the camp itself. I was sent with my company, accompanied by No. 4 company under Captain Baldwin, to retake a hill from which a body of sepoys had been driven. They had been attacked by the enemy in force; and after a heavy loss were obliged to give way, but the Affghans quickly retreated when reinforcements arrived from camp.

Lieutenant Montgomery, who commanded the company of sepoys who were on piquet on this hill, behaved admirably. He was shot through the arm, while charging one of the assailants with a bayonet, but he never left his post, and refused to go on the sick list; and, although severely wounded, he commanded his company in the next day's action.

It was about eleven o'clock at night when we were sent out to retake this hill, and I got into camp about half-past twelve, having left Lieutenant Pollard and a sub-division of my company on the hill, at the command of Captain Baldwin, in obedience to the request of the officer who commanded the piquet of sepoys which had been sent to relieve those who had suffered so severely. About half-past one, Pollard returned, as his services were no longer required, the enemy not having renewed the attack in that quarter.

At this time the Affghans made an attack, and penetrated some way into the camp. They were, however, met by the Jezailchees,* who quickly drove them back, cutting up a number of them with their long knives. All the troops were of course turned out and kept on the alert. The enemy were firing into the camp from every height that was not absolutely in possession of

* Affghan riflemen in British pay.

our piquets; and their bullets were flying like hail among our tents. The sides of the hill were illuminated in every direction by the constant flashes of their jezails and the muskets of our piquets.

About three o'clock in the morning the fire of the enemy slackened, and when day began to dawn it ceased entirely. Not an Affghan was to be seen on the heights, and we were rather puzzled to imagine what had become of them. The advanced-guard was under the command of Sir Robert Sale, and was composed of three companies of H.M. 9th; three companies of H.M. 13th, and two companies of H.M. 31st; with a troop of horse artillery; Backhouse's mountain-train, and some of H.M. 3rd light dragoons. The march was of a severe description, being for the first four miles through the Tezeen pass, a defile of most formidable character, and over seven hills, the last of which, by name the "Huft Kotul,"* is seven thousand eight hundred feet above the sea. The paths were narrow and diffi-

* From two Persian words, "Huft" seven, and "Kotul" a hill.

cult; in many places mere goat tracks, with yawning precipices on either side, down which many of our baggage animals toppled over, and were lost.

The two companies of the 31st, attached to the advanced guard, were No. 3, of which I had the command, and No. 4 under Captain Baldwin. At daybreak, we moved off our encamping ground, and joined the others in the road leading to the pass. We moved forward in column of sections, according to the seniority of regiments, and entered the pass without seeing any indication of an enemy. We had proceeded about two miles in the defile, when suddenly a long sheet of flame issued from the heights on each side, and a thousand balls came whizzing and whistling about our heads. The hills were lined with the enemy in great force, and they began a most heavy fire. Some of our men dropped, but we did not long give them the opportunity to pepper us at their convenience. Sir Robert soon gave the word for the 13th to ascend and storm the heights on the right, and the 9th and 31st those on the left. Up we went, helter skelter. The hill was very high and precipitous, and not easily ascended at any time; the shot of the enemy, however, quickened our motions, and in a short time we were up and at them. The fire was tremendous; the bullets were hopping and whistling among us in every direction. The enemy were very numerous, and seemed disposed to fight to the last for the possession of the heights. No sooner, however, had our men arrived at the top, than they fixed bayonets, and with a loud hurrah charged the enemy.

The Affghans stood manfully, being encouraged by their leaders; but it was but for a moment—it passed—and they were borne bodily down the hill. Such a smoke and confusion as preceded the charge I never witnessed before, or since; scarcely could I see a yard on either side. The Affghans were shouting their war cry of "Allah il ullah" and reproaching us with various elegant names, such as dogs, kafirs and the like, and assuring us we never should reach Cabul. Some of Captain Broadfoot's sappers, who were with us, gave them as good as they sent in right good Billingsgate. The loss on our side in taking possession of this important post, was much less than could have been expected, but few casualties occurring among our men. An officer of the 9th, was severely wounded; and my subaltern, Lieutenant Pollard, who was always first in a fray, was knocked down and received a severe contusion from a large block of stone, while most gallantly attempting to take a standard. Many Affghans were bayoneted on the summit of this height, and I should like some of those gentlemen who write about the bayonet being a useless weapon, to have seen the execution done by our gallant fellows that day.

There is no weapon like the bayonet in the hands of a British soldier. The Affghans would stand like statues against firing, but the sight of the bristling line of cold steel they could not endure. The bayonet has decided numerous conflicts in all quarters of the globe, and, I doubt not, will decide many more.

Among those of the enemy who fell, was a very portly chief. He was astonishingly fat; and a man of my company, who was a butcher, came up to me, and pointing him out, "Be Jasus, Sir," said my Hibernian friend, smacking his lips with professional gusto, "I never seen a man in such fine condition in my life. Why Sir, he has got my finger deep of fat on his ribs," and he looked quite longingly at the fellow's carcase.

From the pocket of this corpulent individual, one of the men of my company took a long roll of paper, on which was a quantity of Persian writing. He gave it to me, and, on arrival in camp, I forwarded it to the brigade-major, thinking that it might contain some important intelligence. It turned out, however, to be the marriage settlement of his daughter, who appeared by the document, to have entered upon a state of connubial felicity but a few days before the battle, in which her obese progenitor fell.

An officer of the 9th showed me a jezail which he had taken from an Affghan who was killed. It was loaded, and I was astonished at the quantity of charge which it contained. The ramrod, when put down the barrel, extended fully a foot from the muzzle. There must have been four or five times as much powder in the charge as is contained in one of our cartridges.

No sooner had we broken the Affghans, than we kept them on the run along the heights, which are generally in continuous ridges the whole length of the pass. The height on which we were, was commanded by other hills, that were from our position perfectly inaccessible, and from which the

## BATTLE OF TEZEEN.

Affghans, in number about ten thousand, kept upon us a most incessant and galling cross fire. At a particular part of the pass where an opening appeared for the use of artillery, we were ordered by signal from below to lie down, which being obeyed, the howitzers began to throw shrapnel shells over us among the Affghans, who lined the heights which towered above those we occupied.

This situation was to us about the most unpleasant in which we could be placed. The shells kept whistling past about three or four feet above us; and, had one by accident burst before it was intended to do so, no small havoc would have been played among us by our friends The shells were, however, admirably directed, and they soon had the desired effect among the enemy.

The gallant 13th were as successful on their side as we had been on ours. Among the enemy opposed to them, I observed one individual whose bravery was very conspicuous. He carried a large blood-red standard, which trailed on the ground behind him, as he sloped the pole over his shoulder. When the 13th were pushed up the hill, the enemy retired, keeping up during their retreat a desultory fire on the advancing soldiers.

The brave standard-bearer, however, would not leave his post, but continued standing in a very exposed position on the pinnacle of a rock, brandishing his tulwar in his right hand, and daring the soldiers to come on. They did not want much invitation; but the ascent was very steep which rendered them unsteady in their aim. Fifty muskets were fired at the gallant Affghan, who still maintained his place, until three or four of the most active soldiers got within about a hundred yards of him. He then slowly retired, and disappeared behind the rocks. Great was my surprise on seeing him when the soldiers had nearly reached the station he had left, suddenly re-appear, flourishing his sword over his head with the most vehement gestures. The only answer they made was by a discharge of their firelocks at him, but apparently without effect, as he turned leisurely away, and continued to retire slowly up the hill brandishing his sword and his flag until he disappeared over the brow of the mountain. I did not hear whether he subsequently fell or not, but certainly if he did escape, he deserved it for his undaunted bravery.

When we had completely succeeded in driving the

enemy from the range of heights which commanded the pass, I was ordered with my company to retain possession of a hill which commanded a turn in the road, until the main column and baggage had passed, when I was to join the rear guard as soon as it appeared.

During the whole of this successful attack, which resulted in the enemy being completely beaten at all points, on the left heights of the Tezeen pass, Captain Baldwin of H.M. 31st regiment was the senior officer present, and the regiment felt much aggrieved at the omission of that fact in the official account of the action, for if particular credit was due to any individual where *all* did their duty so well, he, as *senior*, was that one.

From my elevated position I obtained a good view of the battle, which raged far and wide on every side, except on the part of the heights of which we had taken possession. The little Goorkhas, who filled the ranks of Broadfoot's sappers, behaved most splendidly. Far in the distance were to be seen small parties of these diminutive warriors, driving strong bodies of the bulky Affghans before them. I saw one little

Goorkha, who was certainly not five feet high, perform a most gallant act. A number of them had attacked an outpost of the enemy, which was commanded by a height in their possession behind it. The sappers, by their well-directed fire, soon drove the detached Affghans from their post to that of their friends above. A chief, who was on horseback, did not retire for some time, but continued bravely at his post. Two or three of the Goork has, however, having approached him unpleasantly near, he turned his horse's head, and gallopped up the eminence on which his men had retreated. The little Nepaulese, whom I have mentioned, ran forward, and taking a long aim at the chief, who was gallopping full speed, at least a hundred yards' distance from him, fired, and tumbled horse and man over and over each other, until they reached the bottom of the hill. The Affghans immediately commenced a furious fire from above to prevent the body of their chief being despoiled ; but the little Goorkha, caring no more for their bullets than if they had been so many snowballs, ran to the spot, and coolly taking out his knife, very deliberately hacked the fellow's head off, bringing that, his sword, and his horse, away in triumph. The horse was a very fine animal, but unfortunately was struck in the shoulder by the Goorkha's ball, which had passed through the man's thigh, and thus brought them down together.

The Affghans had a large body of cavalry in the field, which were charged and utterly overthrown by H.M. 3rd Dragoons and the 1st Light Cavalry. A dragoon, while riding at a chief whose trappings were of the most costly description had his horse shot under him by a pistol from the Affghan. The soldier fell with his charger; but quickly disengaging himself from the disabled animal, he passed his sword through the chief's body. Then vaulting on his horse, he continued the charge with his comrades, and brought the gallant Affghan steed, with his magnificent caparisons, safely into camp.

The Resaldar, or native commandant of Tait's irregular horse, also performed a most splendid action. He had gone with a number of his men round a narrow track, in order to take a large body of Affghan horse in flank. But, on arriving close to them, a broad and deep ravine, which had not before been perceived, was found to intervene between the belligerents. The horses of the sowars* could not get over such a place; but the gallant Resaldar, being mounted on a splendid Arab, made a dash over the yawning gulf, and cut his way right and left through the enemy and back again, before they had recovered from their astonishment. The heroic Mussulman took the leap back and rejoined his men in safety, having killed five Affghans in his desperate charge in less time than I have taken to tell the story. For this achievement he was afterwards very properly rewarded with the decoration of British India.

Dr. Brydon, who was the only individual fortunate enough to escape the massacre of General Elphinstone's force, had been appointed to the medical charge of the 33rd Regiment N.I., and I heard he had another very narrow escape in this engagement. He was sitting on the pole by which a dooly is carried, when a six-pound shot from one of the enemy's guns struck and splintered the bamboo, without injuring him in the least.

Two pieces of artillery, a twenty-four pounder

* Troopers.

## BATTLE OF TEZEEN.

howitzer, and a twelve pounder, which had been placed in the road to dispute the passage were quickly taken; and the artillery men, who were principally renegade Hindostanees, were put to the sword. Akbar Khan's own state tent, also, was taken and burnt. He had prepared a great feast for his chiefs after his anticipated victory; and the beef and bread which were provided in large quantities near his tent were no unwelcome prizes to our hungry men, who laughed with uncontrollable merriment when they witnessed the preparations which had been so unintentionally made for them by the enemy.

The Affghans having been completely routed by the advanced guard and main column, moved to the rear, and made a most furious attack on the rear-guard. Here they were received by Colonel Richmond of 33rd N. I., who commanded in a most masterly manner; and in a short time, finding the day was lost, the hostile army dispersed by different mountain tracks. So utterly were they overthrown, that Akbar Khan himself, we heard, made his escape from the field, accompanied by but one horseman out of the twenty-thousand warriors who had swelled his ranks that morning. When the rear-guard appeared on the road below the hill on which I was stationed, I was called down by signal and joined them. The enemy had amused themselves during the greater part of the time that I occupied the post in firing jingal\* balls at my party. No damage, however, was done by them, as we could easily cover ourselves when we heard the missiles coming. They fired from a great distance having had quite enough of close quarters during the early part of the day.

In this engagement the gallant Major Skinner of H.M. 31st Regiment particularly distinguished himself. He was sent in command of a detachment across the hills towards the valley of Koord Cabul, by a totally different route to that by which the main army proceeded. While executing this dangerous movement in a country so difficult, and imperfectly known, he suddenly found himself in the presence of a part of the Affghan army of immeasurably superior numbers. By a series of most masterly manœuvres, he not only extricated himself from this exceedingly perilous position, but defeated with great slaughter,

\* Large swivels.

and with little comparative loss to himself, a body of the enemy of at least five times his force.

Poor Skinner is now no more. He died on the Himalayah mountains, where he had proceeded for the benefit of his health shortly after the return of the army. The cause of his death was dysentery, contracted during his exertions in this arduous campaign. By his death the service was deprived of a bright ornament, and I of a sincere friend. He was a first-rate officer, and had his life been spared, and opportunity afforded him, he would have achieved no ordinary reputation. Seeming born to command, he was one of that class of men whose reputation lives long after their frail bodies have returned to their parent dust.

After I joined the rear-guard, we had no opposition. From time to time we saw large bodies of the enemy taking their departure over the hills, and sometimes had an opportunity of quickening their motions by sending a shell or two after them. The road was covered with the dead bodies of Elphinstone's unfortunate army, intermixed with those of many Affghans who had fallen that day, and some of whom the camp followers had dreadfully mutilated. The day after the battle, a messenger was intercepted by us from Khodabux Khan, the chief of Tezeen, to his brother in Kohistan. In a letter found on him, the chief mentioned that Akbar Khan and himself had tried to interrupt our progress with twenty thousand men, but that we had accomplished our purpose in spite of them; and that he, therefore, thought the best thing his brother could do was to go to our camp, and try to make peace with us, opposition being now out of the question. Khodabux stated their loss as consisting of about fifty chiefs and seven hundred men killed, and about double that number wounded. He also said that he thought the Feringees must have lost a great number of men, as the battle was long and obstinately contested. His conjectures were however wrong, our casualties being very slight, amounting to only one hundred and eighty-five.

After passing the last hill, there is a narrow defile, called the Tarekee Tungee, between rocks which rise perpendicularly on each side. This place is not much more than two hundred yards in length, but was completely choked with dead bodies. The stench was most horrible in the confined passage; and, although we had become, in a great measure, accustomed to that sort of thing since we left Gundamuck, it was here absolutely insupportable. These bodies were, of course, part of the unlucky Cabul force who had been shot down here by wholesale.

We arrived in camp at Koord Cabul late at night. I was immediately ordered to go on piquet with my company on the Cabul road; and I was certainly never in worse humour for anything of the kind in my life. I was completely knocked up, having been engaged the whole day with the enemy, climbing up and down hills; awake all the night before, having had to proceed from the camp to succour the piquet which was attacked, as I have before described; nor had either I or my men tasted a mouthful of food for upwards of thirty hours. Off we started, however, and I received orders to pass any Affghans who might come to my post and seek admittance to the camp. It was expected, indeed, that many of the chiefs would make their submission, who had remained neutral until they should find out which was the stronger party. I posted my sentries, and sat down with

Pollard to smoke a cheroot, having first discussed some huge lumps of half-burnt flesh, which our servants brought to our post, and which they denominated grilled mutton. We were hungry enough to make no objections, by whatever name they might choose to call this dog's-meat-looking stuff. During the night, my men also had food brought to them.

Some of our friends soon appeared and wanted to come in. The greater part of the rascals had evidently been fighting against us that day. Their horses were covered with sweat and dirt, and their housings torn and disarranged. The men, too, seemed knocked up, and altogether anybody might discern they had lately been at no easy work. Nevertheless, they were passed in according to orders. I was dreadfully sleepy, and how the sentries managed to keep themselves awake was above my comprehension, for I am sure that I visited them, and gave every order in a state of semi-somnambulism.

From the heavy sleep which soon overcame me, I was only aroused by the click, click, clicking, of the loosening of the tent pegs, which were being struck, and by the busy hum of the camp below,

## KOORD CABUL PASS.

which informed me that morning had arrived, and that we must be up and stirring. As the only toilet we had to perform was to rub our eyes, much time was not wasted in that employment. I was dreadfully stiff and sore from the loose stones on which I had been lying all night. So fatigued had I been, that the night appeared not to have exceeded more than five minutes in duration. I had, notwithstanding, visited my sentries several times and inspected the reliefs, and I had burned a large hole in my cloak from my lighted cigar falling on it, when I was suddenly overcome by sleep.

We formed part of the rear-guard, and moved off at about nine o'clock A.M., after shooting about fifty baggage animals, towards the pass of Koord Cabul. The entrance of this defile is about a mile from the encamping ground in the valley of the same name. On entering the pass, we were all struck with astonishment: we thought we had seen before as formidable places as could by any possibility exist, but they were absolutely nothing in comparison with this almost impregnable defile. It was only necessary to cast one glance on the stupendous heights which, towering to a vast height one over the other, commanded us in front, in the rear, and on both flanks, to make us feel our utter insignificance, and the weakness of human power where the strong hand of nature is stretched forth to arrest its progress. To mount these heights was next to an impossibility. One man on their summit was more than a match for five hundred in the narrow pass below. By a few strokes of a sledge hammer on the enormous masses of rock, which projecting over the pass, seemed to totter in mid air, whole battalions in an instant might have been overwhelmed in one common destruction.

Akbar Khan had determined originally to meet us here and to decide the fate of Cabul. He had neglected no artificial means to render the natural difficulties of the way still more insuperable. Strong barricades of stone were erected across the path between the heights; and on these themselves, sungah surmounted sungah, from under cover of which a most murderous fire might be kept up on all parts of the pass by the defenders, with little comparative risk to themselves. The pass is very winding, so that at every turn all sides of an invading army are assailable at once. It was originally formed no doubt by the river which runs along it, and which we had to cross no less than six and twenty times during this day's march. Fortunately Akbar Khan's better judgment was overruled by the turbulent spirits under him. When the halt in the Tezeen valley was forced upon our army, by the condition of the cattle, the Affghans, who were carefully watching our motions, attributed it either to hesitation or to fear. Khodabux Khan, the chief of Tezeen, sent word to Akbar that we had suffered considerably in our previous engagements, and were reduced to such extremities that we could neither advance nor retreat, and that therefore he ought to come down, and, concentrating his whole force for the attack, to cut us to pieces where we were. Akbar reluctantly complied with the demand of his chiefs, and, moving from his stronghold, met us in the Tezeen pass, and Huft Kotul. The result was, as I have before described, the utter annihilation of his army. So great was the panic excited among the Affghans by the events of that day, that our passage through the most difficult pass of the whole was undisputed. Some few shots were dischargd at the rear-guard but nothing more.

The scene within the pass was of the most heart-rending description. Elphinstone's army had suffered most dreadfully here, and the dead lay in heaps. They seemed, indeed, in some places, to have been mowed down by whole battalions. They had been preserved in the snow, and their ghastly faces often apparently turned towards us, seemed to call upon their fellow-countrymen to revenge their fate.

On many of the bodies we found packets of letters in perfect preservation; and on one, evidently that of an officer, placed next his heart, a small packet containing a long fair lock of woman's hair. Alas! some fond heart, no doubt, still aches for him, whose once manly form still lies unburied in this fatal pass! What a lesson for human pride was this! Some of England's best blood—the officer of rank—the private soldier—and the humble camp follower,—lowest of the low, all lay here in one undistinguishable mass of slain!

Poor fellows, their gallantry deserved a better fate. They fought and died like soldiers, while gaunt famine was preying upon their very vitals. They did all that men could do: but hunger and cold they could not overcome. Of the fatal mismanagement which led to the disastrous situation which cost so many brave men their lives, I shall, at present, say nothing, as it is my intention to make a few observations regarding it hereafter. It appears to be pretty well understood in England.

On emerging from the Koord Cabul pass, we found a quantity of shot and shells which had been abandoned by the discomfited Affghan army during their precipitate flight. Our camp was about five miles from the pass, and it was with the greatest difficulty that I kept myself partially awake until we arrived at Bootkak, so completely was I knocked up with the exertions of the last four or five days. I was continually falling into a slumber while on my horse, from which I was only aroused by nodding my head against his neck, or by the poor brute's stumbling, on one occasion of his doing which, I was thoroughly awakened by getting rather a heavy fall. On arriving in camp, I found my tent pitched, and throwing myself down on the ground, without taking off a single article of clothing, I went fast asleep, and never awoke until the bugle sounded the next morning for the march towards Cabul.

We were joined during this march by many Affghan chiefs, who professed themselves our best friends, although we knew well enough they had been fighting as hard as they could against us until they found it was of no use. We were also met by some of the regiments of Shah Soojah's force, with bands playing, and by many of the Kuzzilbashes. Our soldiers seemed rather sulky with our Affghan friends, who, though they professed so much for us, probably lent a hand towards the late tragedy; and, had our circumstances been otherwise than they were, would doubtless have done their best to have served us in the same manner. It was, however, necessary to get supplies, which would have been difficult but for the assistance of these new allies, and when we arrived in camp at Cabul I heard that we had but two days' provision for the army left.

We encamped about three miles from the city of Cabul, which was deserted by the greater number of the inhabitants, who had also removed most of their valuables when they heard the result of the battle of Tezeen. Sir Richmond Shakspeare proceeded with a body of about eight hundred Kuz-

BALA HISSAR, OR CITADEL OF CABUL.

Published by Henry Colburn Great Marlborough Street. 1844.

zilbashes to a fort some marches off, and was fortunate enough to recover the whole of the prisoners taken by the Affghans from the late unfortunate force, with the exception of Captain Bygrave, who however was very generously sent back in a few days afterwards by Akbar Khan, who, finding his game was up, nobly observed, it would be a poor revenge on his part to keep a solitary individual from his friends, and bade him go and join his countrymen. I believe he even furnished him with the best escort his altered fortunes would allow to protect him on the road.

The Bala Hissar was taken possession of by a detachment from the different regiments of the army on the day of our arrival, and the British flag hoisted on the highest pinnacle of the ramparts.

Many brass and iron cannon, in all seventy or eighty pieces, were found inside. Some were very beautifully ornamented with various figures of fish and other animals, while the muzzles were shaped like alligators' heads which, when they were fired, would seem to emit thunder and flame. One of the pieces was about eight feet long, made of iron, of an octagon shape and rifled. This extraordinary cannon would carry a three or four pound ball, and was doubtless an excellent and most destructive mountain gun. It was made in a remarkably light and tasty manner. There was also a very beautiful Dutch brass twenty-four pounder among them. How Mynheer got there, I cannot imagine; but it certainly was as fine a piece of ordnance as I have ever seen. We also searched all the forts in the vicinity, and found a most miscellaneous collection of articles in all of them. Numberless packets of letters and office papers, wearing apparel, hair brushes, and all sorts of things belonging to the late unfortunate force were discovered. Among other things was found the copy of the will of Captain S., of our own regiment, who died near Pesh Bolak. This will had been sent for from lower India at that time; but the dâk in which it was forwarded had been intercepted by the enemy. Singularly enough, that after having gone through Akbar's hands it should again turn up and fall into those of the deceased's friends. Quantities of grain and lucerne grass, twisted into ropes for winter's consumption, were found, and such of our cattle as were now

CITY AND VALLEY OF CABUL.

Published by Henry Colburn, Great Marlborough Street. 1844.

## THE BALA HISSAR. 237

left, found themselves at last in the midst of plenty.

The city of Cabul is very extensive, and the houses are far superior to those which I have ever seen in any Indian city. With the exception, however, of the principal choke* and bazaars, the streets are exceedingly narrow and dirty. The Bala Hissar is a strong citadel surrounded by a high wall and bastions of stone work, and encompassed by a wet ditch, the formidable character of which is much increased by the banks being, for some distance from the fortress, of a very boggy nature. But there is this fault about the stronghold: it is too extensive and would require a great number of men to defend it properly. It is built at the foot of a high mountain which completely commands it, but across which is built a strong wall, strengthened by small towers at intervals. Doubtless it would be exceedingly difficult to take this mountain, if properly defended; but it would require a very large force to perform that service. However, the Bala Hissar with all its faults and disadvantages of situation and fortification, would with

* Market-place.

a British force, be perfectly impregnable to any oriental army as long as provisions for the garrison could be obtained. General Sale defended Jellalabad, which possessed nothing like the advantages, and was liable to ten times as great disadvantages as the Bala Hissar at Cabul, with a force not more than one-fourth the strength of that army, which retreated without making an attempt at holding the latter.

A few days after we had taken possession of Cabul, the gallant General Nott arrived with the Candahar army. He had retaken the fortress of Ghuznee, and beaten the enemy in several obstinate engagements. Shortly after his arrival, a division composed partly of his, and partly of our army, was sent into Kohistan, under the command of Major General M'Caskill. They proceeded to Istaliff, where an Affghan army of some strength was lying, and under guard of which a vast number of the inhabitants of Cabul had collected their families and valuables. On summoning the Affghan general, he replied, that so far from wishing to avoid an engagement, he had intended to proceed to Cabul in order to cut up all the Feringees there, and the division having advanced upon him, would save him the trouble of going so far to annihilate them. An engagement, of course, followed the gasconade of this doughty hero. His army was utterly overthrown with immense slaughter, and the city with an enormous quantity of valuables, such as bales of cloth, silks, satins, and about four thousand women and children fell into the hands of M'Caskill's division. The brave Colonel Taylor and his gallant corps, H.M. 9th covered themselves with glory, and their bright example was emulated by the 26th regiment, N. I., which is one of the best regiments in the Company's army.

A guard was placed over the females and children, and they were as safely protected in the European camp, as if they had been among their own friends. Negociations were entered into with one of the Affghan chiefs, to whom they were all safely delivered over without ransom of any kind. This moderation on our part must have surprised our savage enemies, whose conduct would have been so dissimilar had they gained the day. The city itself was burned; and there being not sufficient carriage even for necessaries, all the valuable plunder shared the same fate, it being impossible to take it away. In about ten or twelve days, the division marched back, and joined us again at Cabul.

It was impossible to find out what were the intentions of the General regarding this city. For some days nothing was done, and the owners of the shops in the chokes began again to display their wares for sale. Quantities of horses and fruit were also brought into our camp for the same purpose. The Cabul ponies are very stout and strong animals, and have a pleasant ambling pace. They are very sure-footed among the hills, and would almost climb up a ladder. On the plains, however, they stumble dreadfully. The horses are fine looking animals with great bone, but are heavy and sluggish in their pace. Were they crossed with the Arab, I have no doubt that the progeny would be very fine.

The grapes which are grown at Cabul are, I suppose, the finest in the world, both in flavour and size. Apples and pears were also common enough, and were greedily devoured by us, such fruit not being obtainable in lower India; but, compared with those of England, they are the most tasteless and insipid things imaginable. Eating the apples always put me in mind of chewing the pith of an elder tree.

Six iron nine-pounders having been found in the Bala Hissar, it was determined to destroy them, as they were not worth taking away; and, indeed, their immense weight would have rendered it difficult to do so. Some of my readers may probably wonder how heavy guns are destroyed in the field, I shall, therefore, describe the manner in which these were burst. They were each loaded with, I believe, twenty pounds of powder, on which were rammed two or three round shot, and the muzzle of every gun was then closely stopped up, by a plug of wood driven into it. Six holes had been dug into the earth in a line, deep enough to bury the guns, muzzle downwards, as far as the touch-holes. The cannons were placed in these, and the earth firmly closed up all round them. They were thus buried in a line in the ground with only the breeches above the surface. A train having been laid with a branch to the touch-hole of each, it was fired by an officer who lighted a slow match at the end of it, and then mounting his horse gallopped to a safe distance. When the explosion took place, the guns were burst to atoms.

After we had been at Cabul about a fortnight, a force of four companies of the 31st regiment, and of some detachments from the different native corps, was ordered one evening to be in readiness to march on the following morning into the city. The object was not stated, but we could form a pretty good idea of what we were to do, and the result proved that our expectations were correct. We proceeded the next morning, and blew up all the principal chokes and bazaars where Sir W. M'cNaghten's head and others had been exposed, and set fire to the city in many places. The houses were of course gutted in a very short time, and bales of cloth, muslins, fur cloaks, blankets, and wearing apparel of every description were turned out and destroyed. Quantities of English belts and pouches, and a variety of other articles which they had taken from Elphinstone's force were also discovered. Some of the men found a number of English cases of hermetically sealed grouse, and other meats, on which, as may be imagined, they had a fine feast. In blow-

## DESTRUCTION OF CABUL.

ing up the bazaars, some of our officers and men received severe contusions from the falling beams.

We continued the work of destruction until night closed upon us, and then returned to camp tired enough. Many of our men looked just like chimney-sweepers from the fire and smoke. On succeeding days other parties were sent, and the city of Cabul, with the exception of the Bala Hissar, and the Kuzzilbash quarter, was utterly destroyed and burned to the ground. An immense deal of property was wasted; but we could not carry it away. The houses were nearly all built of dry light wood, and when once a fire was kindled it would have been impossible to stay the ravaging element. The conflagration lasted during the whole time we remained encamped in the vicinity; and we still saw it when entering the Koord Cabul pass, on our return. A large mosque which the Affghans had built in honour of their success over Elphinstone's army, and called the Feringees' mosque, was also blown up and destroyed.

The weather was now becoming piercingly cold at nights, and on our nocturnal piquets we were half frozen. The higher range of mountains became white crested, and thick black clouds hovering overhead gave token that winter was fast approaching, and warned us to depart before the passes were again filled with snow. In Affghanistan, the transition from summer to winter takes place almost by magic. In one night, perhaps, suddenly the snow falls, and the season and whole face of the country are altogether changed. Winter of the severest and most rigorous kind at once succeeds a hot summer.

We were all anxiously enough looking for orders to retrace our steps now that we had done all that lay in our power to punish the Affghans for their treachery to our unfortunate countrymen. An unwearied career of success had marked our march on Cabul. One blow of the British lion's paw had, as it were, changed the whole aspect of affairs over which our enemies had so lately rejoiced. The prisoners in their hands had all been rescued in safety; every city they possessed had been taken and destroyed; and Akbar Khan himself, the master-spirit of the whole nation, was a fugitive, with a price upon his head, and with scarcely a single follower. But a few months before, and how different was the state of our affairs! An army beaten at all points, and utterly annihilated; all the fortresses, with one exception, which we had taken, again in the hands of the enemy, and that solitary post but weakly garrisoned, and besieged by a large army under Akbar Khan himself. Add to this, the independent natives of lower India were looking on the operations of our relieving army with anxious suspense, and stood ready, the moment they should hear of our suffering the slightest repulse, to pounce upon the dominions of the now no longer invincible Feringees, which the formation of our army had absolutely drained of soldiers.

Our successes turned the scale, and produced the greatest moral effect on the natives. They now saw, that however the sun of our prosperity might be obscured by adverse clouds, yet surely would its beams again break forth with additional splendour from the dark chaos in which it had, for a brief period, been obscured.

## CHAPTER X.

General Elphinstone's retreat — Errors committed — Dr. Brydon—His perilous escape—General Pollock issues orders to retrograde—Difficulties of the march—The Koord Cabul pass—Conveyance of an Affghan trophy—Narrow escape of a courier—Jugdulluck—Engagement with the Affghans—Luxurious repast — Gundamuck—Futtiabad—Jellalabad.

It is difficult for any person, who has been in Affghanistan and seen anything of its people, to imagine how any set of men could have proposed the retreat of our unfortunate force, or counselled the plans by which it was preceded. It would scarcely be supposed that while the army was encamped outside the town, the provisions and stores of every kind were kept in magazines almost without guard in the centre of the city, absolutely placed, by the fatal security in which the British leaders were lulled, in the very grasp of a crafty and warlike enemy. How the Affghans themselves must have ridiculed the credulity which gave them such a chance! We call *them* barbarians—would *they* have been guilty of such folly?

When the Affghans took advantage of the temptation which was placed in their way, what did the British leaders do?

Any one would imagine that having been opposed by no regular army, but merely by the hostile population of a city which had not struck a blow in its defence when first captured, it would have been no very difficult matter for a British force to retake the stores at once, and, by shooting some hundreds of the insurgents, at one blow to put an end to the insurrection. Or, if the force was not sufficient to have crushed the rebellion in the bud, what hindered their throwing themselves into the Bala Hissar, and seizing all the provisions in the city, which were ample, and would have enabled them to have held out until the snow melting from the passes, might open a way for reinforcements: or failing that, by which they themselves might retreat with no great loss? General Sale and his gallant band retreated through the same passes, a little earlier in the season, without a very severe loss, although constituting not more than a fourth part of the number of the Cabul army, and throughout opposed to the fierce assaults of the Affghans. The soldiers of the force which were annihilated, were of the same quality as General Sale's, and would have done as much had they had the same commanders. But Sale, Denny and Monteath were hosts in themselves, for however trying the circumstances, the troops under them felt confidence in their leaders, whom they knew to be equal to any emergency.

There was one plan, which any person of sense might foresee, would doom the whole force to destruction. It was, without striking a blow for the recovery of their stores, to attempt a retreat through passes choked up by snow, without food, without ammunition, or the means of carrying it, and where even were it to be had, the cold was so intense as to prevent the troops from using their arms with any effect. This was the plan which the leaders determined to adopt. We can only ascribe their determination to insanity. The man who throws himself from the monument is but equally deranged, and his madness only destroys *himself*, while unfortunately that of the British leaders destroyed thousands of men who, had they been better led, would have beaten any force the Affghans could have brought against them. How many brave and talented officers, alas! were in this unfortunate affair lost to their country, and how bitter must their reflections have been, while the work of disorder and destruction was going on, that they were sacrificed by the downright folly of those who were so totally unfit to command them!

The catastrophe forms a dark page in the history of England's glory; but the brilliancy of the succeeding operations has thrown a halo round it, by which the gloom is more than partially dispelled.

The sufferings of the unfortunate army, while attempting to force a retreat, were unparalleled. Dr. Brydon's account of the miseries they experienced was enough to make the most stony heart bleed. The feet and hands, he said, of the unfortunate sepoys being completely frost-bitten, looked like pieces of burnt wood; and the idea of their using their arms was a farce, for they could not use their limbs, but were cut down without the possibility of resistance. They dropped and died by hundreds in the road; and, when morning broke on the bivouacs of the wretched army, hundreds of little hillocks in the snow, marked where as many brave men lying down to rest their wearied limbs had found their graves under the cold winding sheet in which during the night the icy winter had enveloped them. A soldier of the 44th who had been on the retreat, informed me that, being wounded and lying in the road, he heard Akbar Khan tell his men not to blunt their knives upon the Hindostanees, as they were sure of dying of cold, but to follow up the Europeans like bloodhounds, and give them not a moment's rest until they were fairly worn out and destroyed, to a man.

The army, although without food, and having lost nearly two-thirds of its numbers, preserved some appearance of organization, until they arrived at Jugdulluck. The enemy were hot on their heels in resistless force, and Generals Elphinstone and Shelton with some other officers, who had proceeded to a fort to hold a conference with Akbar Khan, for the purpose of trying by some convention to avert the horrors which were going on, were detained by him as prisoners. To this circumstance they owed their lives, which would otherwise have inevitably been lost.

The command now devolved upon Brigadier Anquetil, who fell gallantly fighting at the head of the soldiers, who most nobly rallied under him. Had he earlier succeeded to the command, and had his life been spared, the results might have been different. In the narrowest part of the Jugdulluck pass, the soldiers maintained some order, but the camp followers, being seized with a panic, made a rush to the front and again to the rear, and being very numerous they became mixed up with the men, many of whom were trodden down and destroyed. From that moment, the rout became general, and it was no longer a fight but a massacre. Some of the Europeans of the greatest physical strength and power of endurance, with a few officers, among whom was the gallant Captain Souter, still kept together, and although without ammunition and having been destitute of food for some days, they made their way two marches farther until near Gundamuck, when they were all, with one or two exceptions, destroyed by numberless fresh tribes who attacked them. These men must have made a fearful struggle for their lives. It was wonderful to look upon the passes, and difficult to believe that human beings could have borne up against their accumulated miseries so long. What would not such soldiers have effected had they been ably commanded! No enterprise would have been too arduous, no attempt too desperate for them.

Dr. Brydon himself owed his life to the generosity of a native of Hindostan. His horse had been shot under him, and at the time of the utter disorganization of the force, he was making the best of his way on foot along the road, when he was accosted by an old subadar\* who was bleeding by the side of the path, but with one hand holding the bridle of his horse which stood beside him. "Sahib," said this noble fellow, "my hour has come: I am wounded to death and can ride no longer. You, however, still have a chance, take my horse which is now useless to me, and God

---

\* A native officer of a sepoy regiment.

send you may get into Jellalabad in safety." Brydon mounted the horse which was shortly afterwards shot through the loins, while his sword was broken by a large stone hurled at him by a Ghilzee. While in this condition, he was attacked by an Affghan horseman who wounded him in several places. The poor fellow was quite overpowered by fatigue, starvation, and loss of blood, and he fell forward on the pummel of his saddle at which were holsters, but no pistols. The cowardly Affghan, however, mistaking his movement, believed he was going to draw a pistol, and wheeling round his horse galloped away with all speed. The Doctor, now relieved from his enemy, had still sufficient endurance and courage left to determine to make every effort to push on. His wretched nag, sorely wounded, could scarcely go out of a shuffling trot, and he himself was barely able to sit in the saddle. Wonderful to relate, after twenty hair-breadth escapes, he succeeded in reaching Jellalabad, where he had no sooner arrived than the poor animal, which had been the means of saving him, dropped down dead. Had this occurred an hour or two before, he must have been lost, for walk he could not. Strange also was it, that many officers and men riding on capital horses passed him on the road; and yet he, so wretchedly mounted, was the only one who got in. The determination and persevering firmness which he displayed are worthy of the greatest credit. It is in situations like these that we find out what men are made of.

About the middle of October, the expected orders to retrograde were issued by General Pollock. A division under the command of General Sale was ordered to proceed, without baggage, over the hills by a mountain path, by which they would be enabled to turn the Koord Cabul pass, and take possession of the heights. The succeeding day our division followed, having in charge a most enormous train of baggage. I never shall forget the confusion caused on leaving our encamping ground, the numerous camels and other baggage-animals being jammed in the narrow road, on either side of which was a morass. By some mismanagement, they had been allowed to get ahead of the column, and the delay, heat and dust, were intolerable. It was several hours before we could proceed on our way. At last, we managed to get through the press, and proceeding on our

## THE KOORD CABUL PASS. 255

march, encamped in the evening near Bootkak, about three miles from the pass of Koord Cabul.

I was on piquet that night, and fully expected an attack; but, with the exception of a few shots fired at the sentries, all was quiet. The next day I was again on the rear-guard through the Koord Cabul pass, and a most fatiguing day we had of it, with the baggage of two divisions to protect and keep together. In addition to this were about forty pieces of brass artillery which we had captured, and which were to be taken to India as trophies. About two thousand cripples who had been found in Cabul, and who had been sepoys and camp followers with Elphinstone's army, were also with us, mounted on elephants, jackasses, bullocks, and every beast of burden which we had been able to procure for them. The unfortunate wretches had all lost their feet or hands from frost bites, and had subsisted after the departure of the army by begging from the inhabitants of Cabul. They would on our arrival in India be pensioned by a large subscription, which had been raised for the purpose among the European residents. The sepoys were entitled, in addition, to a pension from the East India Company.

Sale's division kept the heights until the main column of our division had defiled through the pass, when they were relieved by our men. It was late in the evening when the rear-guard reached the encamping ground, in the valley of Koord Cabul; and when I went to my tent I found I was the only officer in camp. The whole regiment was on the heights, from which it took them some hours to descend.

In consequence of the pass having been turned, we were not molested on this march, and during the night we were also tolerably quiet. The next day I was with the main-column, and for my sins, I suppose, was ordered with a sub-division of my company to take charge of, and get into camp at Tezeen, a large brass twenty-four pounder howitzer, which was one of the trophies. Lieutenant Pollard had likewise charge of a gun with the other sub-division. Never shall I forget the purgatory through which I had to pass in getting this vile piece of ordnance to the encamping ground. To drag it I had four half-starved oxen, the most self-willed and obstinate of brutes.

They had never been accustomed to a yoke; and even had they been so, it would have required at least a dozen of them to drag such a heavy cannon properly.

To add to my distresses, I had no bullock-drivers, but two classies* were ordered for that duty, who knew as much of the art of bullock-driving, as I did of playing the fiddle. The obstinate oxen had as mortal an aversion to Europeans as their countrymen the Affghans; and whenever the soldiers came near they charged at them most furiously. It was about half an hour before I got them to start at all, and I only then managed it by making some of the soldiers get behind them and twist their tails, while the classies stood at their heads and belaboured them with bamboos, giving utterance at the same time to the most vituperative abuse, to which the men in the rear added a little gentle persuasion with the points of their bayonets.

After a few plunges and kicks, off they went at a great rate, with their tails erect in the air. We kept them at it by means of an occasional dig

* Native tent-pitchers.

with the goads we had found so effective, but, as we had no means of guiding them, they soon got off the road, and were brought up by some rocks. My men had to set to work and drag the gun back into the path, and the former scene was again enacted until we arrived at the Huft Kotul, from which there is a terrific descent by a narrow and winding path, covered with large loose masses of stone. I had no drag ropes, and how to get the gun down I could not tell. I was fairly puzzled, until one of the men suggested, that as we had no drag ropes to hold on by, we should fasten the oxen behind the gun, and letting it run down the slope. the cattle pulling behind would prevent its going down too fast, in which case the carriage would be broken to pieces. No sooner said than done. There were no other means to be pursued, and accordingly we took the animals from the front, and hooking them on behind, started the gun happy-go-lucky down the precipitous descent. For some time it went steadily enough; the oxen pulling manfully against the weight which was dragging them down backwards. In a short time, however, the slope became more abrupt, the gun increased its speed, and at last, the oxen losing their footing, it thundered like an avalanche down the hill amid a cloud of dust and a shower of falling stones, and throwing the unfortunate animals out of the yokes, arrived at the bottom with a crash that might have been heard a mile off, and ran with the velocity which it had acquired in its descent, like a self-acting engine, for about a hundred yards along the road below.

Nothing was broken; the carriage being fortunately made excessively strong. Had it not been so I never could have got the gun into camp, not having been able to procure any of the necessary tackle. We had several such descents to make, which we accomplished in the same manner; while on the corresponding ascents the gun was pushed up by the soldiers behind, the bullocks pulling in front. The whole day had passed, and night was closing in, when I arrived with my treasure at the last descent. As bad luck would have it, this time the gun ran off the road, when nearly at the bottom of the hill, and upset in a ravine. We were now in a pretty mess, and to add to our comfort, a body of the enemy, who had been watching our motions from the hills, began firing on us. Fortunately, the howitzer had upset behind some rising ground, which protected my men; but the bullets kept whistling over our heads as thick as hail while we were endeavouring to get the gun again on its wheels and in the road. We effected this in less time than I could have hoped, and had now a comparatively level road through the Tezeen pass into the encamping ground in the valley. We arrived there at about ten o'clock at night; but the main column and rear-guard did not get in until past twelve, having sustained a sharp fight in the pass, where they had been attacked in the darkness by the enemy in great force, with the hope of being able to plunder the baggage. The Affghans were repulsed with great loss, without being able to obtain possession of a single baggage animal.

General Nott, who commanded the rear-division, had a severe engagement here; but, as usual, the enemy were completely defeated. The staunch old warrior, however, was obliged to burst his eighteen-pounder guns, which he had brought up with him from Candahar, and which he boasted he would take back through the passes. He did not then know what the passes were, having advanced to Cabul by a comparatively level country. General Pollock had acted more wisely, having burst two which had been handed over to him by General Nott, at Cabul. General Nott got his two to Tezeen, but found it impossible to take them further. I heard he was in marvellous ill-humour at being obliged to destroy them. Had it been possible to take them on, he was the man to do it.

In the Tezeen pass one of the officers of Nott's force picked up, among several others, a letter directed to me. The cossid * who was carrying the dâk had been intercepted and murdered by the enemy, who had thrown away the letters as useless. By the date, I found it must have been lying there for nearly a month.

The recollection of the next days' march will always affect me with a feeling of sorrow, for it cost me a dear friend—poor Pender of the 31st regiment. He was as noble a fellow and as brave an officer as ever held Her Majesty's commission. We had been most intimate, and at one time lived together. I was subaltern in the company

* Courier.

which he commanded for a long time, and only left it to take the command of another. We were engaged with the same party of the enemy, although on different hills, when he fell.

Both our companies were with the main column; and, as we proceeded along the road which although tolerably wide is commanded by heights on each side within gunshot, parties were detached and stationed on different points, in order to prevent the enemy from molesting the train of baggage which was in our rear.

I was sent to take possession of, and retain until the baggage had passed, a small hill on the left of the road. A large body of Affghans had showed themselves on a second range of heights which commanded the lower ones on the side of the road. Fortunately, there were a number of large rocks on the summit of that of which I took possession, behind which my men were so effectually covered that I lost none, although the enemy kept up a pretty sharp fire on us, which we returned whenever we could get a glimpse of their turbans above the sungahs, behind which they had ensconced themselves.

Poor Pender was not so fortunate. He was

sent up the next hill from my position, and was most hotly fired on by the Affghans during his ascent. He persevered, however, and arrived at the summit, which was completely commanded by the second range of which I have before spoken, and to take possession of which was rendered impossible by the precipices that intervened. There was no cover, and shortly after a corporal of Pender's company was shot dead; another running to pick him up was mortally wounded, and almost immediately afterwards the gallant Pender himself received a ball on his right shoulder, which passed through him, and came out on his left side near the waist.

The shot knocked him some distance down the hill, and the soldiers thinking he was killed ran and picked him up. When they found he was not dead, but severely wounded, they wished to carry him into camp. The brave fellow, however, would not leave his post, but ordered them to lay him down on a bank near the top of the mountain. After a short time he became quite stiff, and some of the men took him down the hill and carried him into camp, while his company, under the command of a sergeant, retained their post until the baggage had passed, after having dislodged the enemy from their position by a well-directed and steady fire. They met with some more casualties in performing this service, but I do not remember the number.

As soon as I got into camp, I hastened to Pender's tent. His wound had just been dressed, and he was in excellent spirits, only regretting that he had been unable to get at close quarters with the enemy, and that he was disabled from leading his company through the Kyber pass, where we expected to have a severe action, as it was hardly to be expected that the Affghans would let us depart through so difficult an outlet, without having a parting fling at us for doing so much mischief in their country.

Although Pender was a man of most athletic form, and of powerful constitution, he could not rally from the effects of the severe wound he had received, but died within a month. Thus in a paltry skirmish an officer was lost to the service, who possessed every requisite qualification for deeds of the most brilliant character. His mind bore up to the last, and it was only his undaunted courage that kept him alive so long.

We were encamped at a place called Seerbaba, which we had passed on our advance upon Cabul, without halting. It was during this march and the next, which I have before described as having been made in one day, that I was with the rear-guard under the command of the gallant Major Skinner. The encamping ground is of a singular character, being a small circular valley which, surrounded by heights, appears on looking down from them, to resemble the interior of a gigantic punch-bowl. It was, of course, necessary to have strong piquets posted on the heights, from which the enemy might have greatly annoyed us during the night. Captain Baldwin saved the life of a poor courier in a most singular manner at this place. He was ordered for piquet with his company, and, on arriving at the summit of the hill to which he was posted, they came suddenly upon two Affghans who had another man down on the ground between them, and were preparing to cut his throat. They were too much engaged in their pleasant occupation to heed the approach of the soldiers, who immediately fired at the rascals and knocked them over. The poor devil who had been in their power came running up with the most vehement expressions of gratitude to his rescuers. He informed them that he was a Cossid, who had been intercepted by the two ruffians who were shot, and at the moment when Captain Baldwin and his party appeared they had a knife at his throat; one moment later, and it would doubtless have been cut most effectually, the Affghans never doing such things by halves.

The next day, the whole of the 31st regiment was ordered for the rear-guard under the command of Colonel Bolton. The enemy attacked the piquets when they were withdrawn pretty sharply as they descended from the heights. They did not, however, venture to come down, and we were unmolested below. Owing to the steepness of the hills over which we had to drag the guns, the march was tiresome and fatiguing. The half-starved horses could scarcely move, and the wretched condition of the worn-out camels obliged us to shoot them by scores as they dropped down by the way. The property with which they were loaded was, of course, burned to prevent its falling into the hands of the enemy.

We arrived at Kuttasung rather late in the

evening, desperately tired; and the enemy were good-natured enough to leave us alone during the night. The fact was, they had been so constantly beaten with heavy loss in all their attempts on us that they began to lose heart, and allowed us to pass through places unopposed, where they might have seriously obstructed our progress without much loss to themselves.

The next day we arrived at Jugdulluck again, without opposition, although the enemy occasionally shewed themselves far out of our reach on the heights, apparently watching our motions with great interest. We knew pretty well that they would have a slap at us next day in the pass, and got ourselves ready for work. We were not deceived in our expectations, for an action took place, which, for its duration, was nearly as sharp as any in which we had been engaged.

During the night, the enemy were pretty quiet, only amusing themselves by firing a few desultory shots at the piquets, for the benevolent purpose, it may be presumed, of keeping them awake on their posts, lest they might be surprised.

In the morning, I was ordered with my company as a guard over the guns, and had an opportunity of seeing Captain Alexander of the horse artillery make some exceedingly pretty shots. This officer was an excellent marksman, and I had before on several occasions had the pleasure of seeing him knock over many of the enemy with some well-directed shells dropped nicely in among their masses.

The advanced guard passed through the defile, having without a great deal of opposition detached parties on different points of the heights. Our numbers were, however, too small to be able to do more than keep possession of a few of the most essential. The main column with which I was, followed closely after them, occasionally halting on the march to throw a shrapnel shot at the enemy, whenever they showed themselves. The Affghans remained almost inactive, until the rear-guard appeared in the pass, when they attacked them most furiously, in the expectation, no doubt, of getting a good haul at the baggage which they escorted. Many and desperate were the attacks which they made on the long line of camels; but, owing to the judicious positions in which parties had been detached in various parts along the pass, from the advanced guard and main column, they were repulsed in all their attempts with great loss.

The artillery pushing on by the direction of Brigadier Monteath, emerged from the pass, and obtained possession of the raised *plateau* of ground at the mouth of the gorge. This I have before mentioned as being the site so judiciously chosen by the same commander for strengthening the rear-guard, by halting the main column and effecting a junction for the protection of the train of baggage on our advance some weeks before. From this position, the guns were brought to bear upon the enemy, and did great execution among them. They still obstinately contested the fight, until the baggage train was safely through the pass. Finding they had no chance left of getting anything but hard knocks from the gallant rear-guard, and, having already experienced a heavy loss, they then gave up the day without having obtained possession of a single article of baggage. We continued our march without farther opposition. Occasionally a bullet or two would whistle over the column, and a few casualties occurred, but nothing of any consequence; and just as it was getting dark that evening we arrived at Soorkab, where we encamped.

I was sent on piquet to a high hill some distance from the camp, as soon as we got in, without having time to obtain anything to eat, although I had tasted nothing since the preceding day.

We were, however, so accustomed to constant privations, that we esteemed ourselves especially lucky if we got one meal in twenty-four hours. I now often thought how I used to grumble and scold my servants in cantonments if they were five minutes late in preparing my tiffin, or dinner, and how little I then imagined that I should know what it was to be unable to procure food, excepting in the smallest quantities, and of the worst description, for days together.

I had saved a bottle of port wine from my stock, with the determination of drinking the same to the good health of the Affghans when I should get safely through the Kyber pass, on our return. My determination of not drinking it, however, until then, had, like Bob Acre's courage, been daily oozing away. I began to consider that I might be knocked over before I could get through, and then I should never have the satisfaction of enjoying it at all. Captain N—, who was on piquet with me, suggested that it would be a remarkably good opportunity of drinking it, after having come safely through the Jugdulluck, as perhaps I might not have such good luck again. Accordingly, I sent down for it, and one of my servants bringing me a plate of mutton chops from the mess, N— and I sat down and discussed this treat, and gladdened the hearts of some soldiers, who had been very attentive in clearing away the stones from the place on which we purposed sleeping, by a glass each of the inspiriting beverage.

Talk of luxuries, I never in my life experienced so great a one as I found in this glass of wine and plate of tough chops, while I sat shivering near our watch-fire on the cold hill-side, weary, hungry, and exhausted. I was in better humour after it than I had been during the whole campaign; and, as the Affghans did not molest us, I slept most soundly, and woke next morning refreshed and with a light heart from my hard bed.

I was again on the rear-guard, and although various parties of Affghans showed themselves upon the heights, they made no attempts at hostilities, and we arrived without opposition at Gundamuck, where a force had been left in an entrenched camp, when we marched on to Cabul.

Neither letter nor intelligence of any kind had

reached me during our absence, with the exception of that found in the Tezeen pass. A packet, however, awaited me here of most portentous bulk. There were about thirty letters in it, and I was really quite at a loss which to peruse first. With great perseverance, however, I managed to get through all of them, and they supplied me with reading for a week. I used to amuse myself on an outpost by decyphering the crossed and recrossed lines, with which the well-filled sheets were covered, and shortened many a weary hour in this employment.

The following day's march brought us again to Futtiabad, where we had buried poor Marshall on our onward march. One or two officers of Elphinstone's army got down as far as this village, after that unfortunate force was destroyed, but were cut up by the inhabitants. General Sale's troops used these fellows rather roughly when *en route* to Jellalabad. The Affghans allowed the advance and main-column to pass unmolested, but when the rear-guard made its appearance they attacked it in force. The officer commanding, finding the rough and broken ground near the village exceedingly unfavourable for the movement of his men, affected

## A RUSE DE GUERRE.

to retreat in a most disorderly manner. This *ruse* had the desired effect. The Affghans followed the troops which they thought were flying from them, to a considerable distance from the village, and across a fine plain, very favourable for the movements of horse. No sooner had they come so far, than a troop of cavalry, which formed part of the rear-guard, making a dash, got in the rear of the enemy, completely cutting them off from their village and the cover of the ravines surrounding it. The infantry also forming up in their front, the deluded Affghans found themselves regularly in a trap, and immediately fell into the greatest disorder; in endeavouring to escape, the plain was covered with the fugitives. The cavalry rode among them in every direction, hacking and hewing right and left with their long sabres, while the infantry kept up a most destructive fire. The exact loss which the enemy suffered I never heard; but an officer who was an eye-witness informed me that the plain was absolutely covered with dead. The troopers cut them down until from fatigue they could scarcely raise their arms. General Sale's troops have always done pretty good execution when the enemy have had the hardihood to attack them, but never did the foe receive a severer lesson than on this occasion.

To Char Bagh was the next day's march, and we accomplished it without molestation of any kind. There is nothing remarkable in this encampment. On the following morning, we reached Jellalabad, and encamped on the further side of the fort, about two miles from the site of our former long standing camp. The officer who had been left in charge of our invalids at this place, had provided a most sumptuous breakfast for all the officers of the 31st. Immediately, therefore, after dismissing our respective companies, we proceeded in a body to B——'s hospitable tent, where whole hecatombs of grilled fowls, mutton-chops, and beef-steaks, and seas of tea and coffee smoking hot, sent up their savoury steams to heaven. Whence he had managed to collect such a quantity of provision, was a riddle to every body; but there it was, and a hearty welcome with it. Of plates, knifes, and forks, there were few or none, but we had been long enough on short commons not to feel particularly fastidious on that score. A fowl was easily divided by four persons respectively seizing the wings and legs, and by a simultaneous pull quartering the unhappy biped. Mutton-chops were devoured by the dozen, and eggs by the score, by each of the guests, until they could fairly hold no more, and were obliged to give in, with many an affectionate glance, nevertheless, on the bountiful supply of delicacies which remained uneaten, and to the like of which we had so long been strangers.

We also had the gratification of receiving a large packet of newspapers from India at this place. In them we read the accounts of our own feats, and the eulogiums pronounced on our success by the good people in lower India. The Governor-General spared no praise in his address to the army, and an order was passed for every individual who had been through this campaign to receive a silver medal, to be worn at the left breast, and bearing on one side the word "Vindex," and on the other "Cabul, 1842." The ribbon was to be of a variety of hues, blended together, in order, as we heard, to be emblematic of the rising sun. This distinction will of course be much prized by every individual; and more especially by the young soldiers, who receiving at the commencement of their military career, a powerful spur to their ambition, will be induced to spare no effort hereafter to distinguish themselves in their honourable profession. I heard many of our men say that they would much rather receive the medal than any sum of money which could be given to them. The medals have not yet been issued; but, doubtless, the Government will spare no pains to reward the good conduct of their troops, by the speedy distribution of the distinction so much coveted, and so well deserved.

## CHAPTER XI.

Destruction of Jellalabad—Passage of the Choota Kyber—
The Kyber pass—A forced march—Peshawur—The Punjab—Mortality among the soldiers—The triumphal arch—
Arrival at Ferozepore—A dâk trip—A storm—Difficulties
by the way—Drunken Seiks—Arrival at Meerut.

AFTER four days' halt at Jellalabad, the fort
and town were, according to orders, set fire to,
and totally destroyed. Large quantities of gunpowder had been placed under the bastions, and
other places of strength, and the sight of the
immense conflagration at night was awfully grand.
Ever and anon, as the fire reached one of the
mines, a vast pillar of flame would be thrown
high up in the air, shaking the earth under our
feet with the concussion, and lighting up the

landscape for miles around, showing the gloomy hills which surrounded us, seemingly looking at the work of destruction with threatening aspect. Suddenly all would again be dark; and showers of falling beams, large stones, and other rubbish, which had been driven up high into the air by the explosions, would be heard rattling in every direction on the ground.

Jellalabad was totally destroyed. Doubtless, the Affghans will spare no pains to repair the damages done by us to this important stronghold, but years must elapse before a city can again spring up from the heap of ruins which we left.

Our outposts and sentries were fired upon pretty sharply during this night, as the destruction of their dwellings probably stirred up the bile of the Affghans in the vicinity. No loss, however, of any consequence was sustained, and the next morning we marched to Ali Boghan, now feeling that we were really on our return, after having got through the greater part of our work. We did not anticipate any opposition until we arrived at the Kyber pass, the country which intervened being of a comparatively easy and level character, in which the Affghans in their reduced state, could make no attempts on us, that would not result in the complete annihilation of their force.

During the next day's march one of our men shot himself. The poor fellow was knocked up with the hardships and privations he had endured, and, in a fit of melancholy, partaking of derangement, determined to stand it no longer. He told some of his comrades that he would destroy himself; but they thought that if he really intended to do so he would have said nothing about it. However, he obtained leave from an officer to leave the ranks for a short time, and, sitting down on a stone by the road, he put the muzzle of his musket to his breast, and pulling the trigger with his foot, having first taken off his boot to enable him to do so, he killed himself in an instant. This man was not badly off. He left a considerable sum of money in government securities; and certainly no one ever suspected him of being likely to commit so rash an act.

Our men were dying very fast of dysentery, a more or less severe attack of which scarcely a single individual in the army escaped. This disease has a very lowering effect on the spirits, as well as on the physical strength, and doubtless the poor fellow's end was to be attributed in a great measure to its depressing influence.

When going through the Choota Kyber, I was unlucky enough to be on the rear-guard. We had in charge nearly all the trophy guns, among which was the great Cazee* of Jellalabad. This unwieldly piece of ordnance was mounted on a most rickety carriage. As the huge wheels slowly revolved on the axle by the efforts of about forty bullocks, which were yoked to the gun, they grumbled and groaned in a most abominable manner, and I expected every moment to see the whole concern break down, the spokes coming half way out of the felloes at every revolution of the wheels, which from the immense weight of the carriage pressing them down, always seemed of an oval rather than of a circular form. We got it along at the rate of about half a mile an hour, until we came to the narrow tungee†

---

* Name of a large gun. There was another cazee at Ghuznee, which was burst by General Nott, its immense weight rendering it impossible to be moved.

† Defile.

itself, the passage of which we found completely choked up by camels standing closely jammed inside the pass. Crowds of baggage animals of every description were gathered together at the mouth of the defile, waiting for a chance of getting through. This it did not seem likely would be effected for a considerable time, as it appeared, on inquiry, that there had not been a move for six hours.

It was about one o'clock when we arrived, and we were halted until five without the line of baggage having shewn a sign of being able to proceed. I got rather sick of this work, and, as getting through the pass was out of the question, I went over the hills to where the stoppage seemed to commence. The reason of it was now very palpable,—an immense iron mortar having been upset in the narrowest part, which completely closed the passage, so that we might have remained until doomsday had I not proceeded to see what was the matter. I instantly set my company to work, and they with great labour succeeded in breaking the limber, righting it being altogether out of the question. They then attached the drag-ropes to the divided parts, and soon drew them out of the pass. The line of camels and other trophy guns now began to stream through regularly enough, but it was five o'clock in the morning before we got into camp at Lalpoora, having been delayed the whole night in the pass.

We had had nothing to eat or drink all the preceding day, and half an hour after we arrived in camp the bugle sounded for us to start off again towards Lundekhanah, which is about eight miles in the Kyber pass. We were completely knocked up, but there was no help for it. Fortunately, my servant had prepared a quantity of fried meat for me when I first got to my tent, which I hastily devoured before falling in; and, after striking my tent and loading my camels, he galloped after the column on one of my horses, with a bottle of tea, for which I had not been able to wait. This was quite a God-send, for I felt dead-beat, and we expected to meet with some serious resistance from the Kyberees in the pass. Had our anticipations proved correct, we should have had some very fatiguing work in climbing over the heights; and to do that sort of thing on an empty stomach is anything but pleasant.

We entered the pass, expecting every moment a volley from the frowning hills on either side; but, to our astonishment, not a shot was heard, nor a Kyberee to be seen. For some time we proceeded, supposing the enemy had thought it prudent to get us well into the pass before they commenced the attack. Still we went on, until we nearly arrived at the encamping ground at Lundekhanah, without a sign of opposition. At last the conviction forced itself on our minds that the Kyberees did not intend to fight. Our men seemed much disappointed, having made up their minds for a fray; but the enemy would not give them a chance. Why they allowed our division to pass unmolested I never could imagine, as those behind were most furiously attacked, and experienced heavy losses.

We got into camp this day rather early, it being a short distance, and the passage undisputed. The next day's march was to Ali Musjid, a very long and tedious journey, highly dangerous from the difficulty and length of the way. When we went through the Kyber, on our advance, we divided the distance from Lundekhanah into two marches, halting at Lalbeg Ghurry, which is about half way between the two places. This was a far wiser arrangement, the pass from Lundekhanah to Lalbeg Ghurry being of the most formidable character, with a very long winding and steep ascent, which the baggage train would surely take many hours to accomplish. The greater part of the force, and most certainly the rear-guards, would probably be detained thereby in the pass all night; when, of course, it would in the darkness be impossible to prevent the enemy from plundering the baggage. It was said that the reason of our not halting at Lalbeg Ghurry was the want of water there, but that must have been a mistake, as we found plenty on a previous occasion, and General Nott halted there afterwards. The worst place in the world to try a forced march is in a difficult pass, and so the divisions after us found, although we were fortunate enough to get through without loss.

We did not anticipate a free passage through the Lundekhanah pass when we started that morning, but to our surprise no enemy appeared. We marched up the ascent with the band playing in front " Away, away to the mountain's brow !" and a variety of other tunes, which had a most

## LOSS IN THE PASS. 285

beautiful effect in this wild scene, and shewed the Kyberees that we were willing to give them due notice of our whereabouts, if they had any wish to try their luck against us. After a most fatiguing march, we got in at night to our encamping ground at Ali Musjid. The rear-guard was very late in arriving, having been detained in the pass; the cattle being completely knocked up by the length and difficulty of the way, and unable to proceed but at the slowest pace. They had some little skirmishing with the Kyberees, who came down when it got dark; but nothing serious took place.

The next day, we continued our route, and, emerging from the Kyber pass, encamped between it and the city of Peshawur. When here, we heard the intelligence of General M'Caskill's division having been benighted in the pass during the long march of which I have before spoken, and of its having been attacked on all sides by the Kyberees in the darkness. A heavy loss of baggage and two guns had been experienced, and many officers and men were killed and wounded. The guns were re-captured the next day, and the great Cazee from Jellalabad, which had broken down in the Lundekhanah pass, was burst, it not being possible to remove it. General Nott, who was in the rear of all, was also furiously attacked; but that staunch old commander gave the enemy good cause to regret their impetuosity, having defeated them with great loss. We heard that he would not attempt the forced march, which had been the sole cause of the losses which the other division experienced; but, wisely halting at Lalbeg Ghurry, was enabled to get his baggage every day into camp, and his guards and piquets posted before nightfall.

On emerging from the Kyber, I pulled off my cap, made a low bow to the gloomy mountains which we had now left behind us, and fervently expressed a hope that I might never be obliged to visit them again. I was quite sick of the sight of hills, and thought the view of the Indian plains must be most enchanting, after the barren and rock-bound country we had left. It was delightful, too, to get through the day's march without hearing ever and anon a bullet whistle by in most unpleasant propinquity to one's person. We were not allowed this time to halt at Peshawur, for the reason, as we heard, that the Seik government regarded us as such desperate fellows, and so accustomed to plunder and free quarters, that there was very little chance of our resisting the temptation of looting* the good city of Peshawur, if we should happen to be encamped near it.

A large Seik army was in the immediate vicinity; but they were desperately afraid of us now that we had come back crowned with victory,— an event so contrary to their expectations. Instead of the impertinence and insolence which they formerly shewed, they were now our best friends, the most obliging fellows imaginable, and bowed and scraped upon all occasions.

On the 1st of November, we encamped about four miles from Peshawur, arriving at the ground by a circuitous route, so as to avoid passing near the city at all. General Avitabili was as hospitable and as civil as ever; and any officer who took the trouble to go to his house might feast *ad libitum* on all sorts of Seik and European delicacies.

At this time poor Pender of the 31st, who received so severe a wound near Seerbaba, still survived, although much reduced. The constant

* Sacking.

moving and shaking of the dooly in which he was carried, and the impossibility of getting proper rest and food, had the worst effects on his frame. He was evidently sinking when we arrived near Peshawur, but rallied again after two or three days' halt, and began to hope that if he could obtain rest for a few days he might survive. On the opinion of the surgeon being asked, he said that if Pender went on with the force he could not survive beyond the first march, the motion of the dooly being certain to kill him in his already reduced state. He seemed himself to have such a strong idea that he should recover, if he could only be quiet for a fortnight or three weeks, and he had so strong an objection to go on with the corps, that by his direction a communication was made with General Avitabili to know if he would give him a room in his house, and shew him attention if he remained behind. This Avitabili kindly promised to do, and the permission of General Pollock having been obtained to the arrangement, at his own urgent request Pender was put into a dooly, and taken to Peshawur. General Pollock refused a solicitation which was made to allow an European soldier to remain behind to attend him; but as Avitabili said that every attention should be showed him, and all his own servants were with him, this, although desirable, did not seem to be absolutely necessary. I saw poor Pender the day before we marched, when he was comfortably located in a room over the gateway, in front of the Seik general's house; and, although he was a perfect skeleton in appearance, he seemed sanguine that he should eventually recover; and asked me to bring him some bottles of wine and spirits next day, as he might require such things when he got well. When I returned to camp late that night, I found that orders had been unexpectedly issued for us to march the next morning, so that I was not able to see the poor fellow again. Accounts afterwards reached us that he had moved on from Peshawur with General Nott's force, and that he had died after the third march, at a place called Nowshera. I have lately heard from Captain Pender of the 62nd Regiment, that his gallant and unfortunate brother was by accident found in a most wretched state by some of the officers of the 41st Regiment. It appeared he had been shamefully neglected by the servants; no one, by his own account, having come near him after we left. Only one domestic was with him, and he would give him nothing to eat but the remains of his own meals of rice. Pender himself was too weak to be able to move, and his other servants must have deserted, having probably first plundered him; for by the same account I heard, that he had no bed, but only an old horse-cloth to cover him. If this account be true, those to whose care he was confided must have behaved most scandalously; as I myself heard General Avitabili say on the last day that I was in Peshawur, that no endeavours should be wanting on his part to make him comfortable. Pender at this time had his own charpoy* and bed-clothes, and seemed to be as comfortable as it was possible for a man in his state to be.

During the time he had then been at Avitabili's (I think three days) he could have experienced no neglect; as, had that been the case, he would have altered his determination of remaining, and have gone on with his regiment, although it was signing his death-warrant to attempt it. Poor fellow, it would indeed appear that he came to a most

* A Hindostanee bedstead.

miserable end; but every arrangement that it was in the power of his friends to make to ensure his comfort, when he determined to remain behind, was made. His gallantry deserved a better fate.

All General Pollock's necessary arrangements having been completed, we marched on the 12th of November from the camp near Peshawur. Our men were very sickly from the effects of the privations and hardships they had undergone. The mortality among them was frightful. We were ordered to push on without making the usual halts, and the fatigue consequent upon this constant marching prevented our sick men from rallying. We had no means of conveyance for them but kajawahs* slung on camels, the rough motion of which, to men in the last stage of disease, many of them suffering from wounds, must have been insupportable. Recovery was out of the question. If it were necessary for the healthy part of a victorious army to push on through a friendly country as if it was flying from an enemy, I do not know why the sick and wounded could not have followed under the

* A kind of rude chair, hung in pairs over the backs of camels.

charge of medical officers in a more leisurely manner, by easy marches, three or four times a-week. Had this plan been adopted, many, many brave fellows, who sank under the constant marching, might have been saved to their country. The 31st lost two more officers on this march,—Lieutenant Sayers, who died of small-pox, and Lieutenant Tritton, of dysentery. We lost also an immense number of men. Some died of small-pox, which had broken out in the camp, but the greater part of dysentery.

Many accounts reached us of the grand preparations which were being made for our reception at Ferozepore by the Governor-General, who spared no pains to express the delight which he felt at our success. A triumphal arch was ordered to be erected on the bridge of boats, by means of which we were to cross the Sutledge. The functionaries, whose business it was to carry out this intention of Lord Ellenborough's, had most decidedly failed in the execution. The boats composing the bridge itself were covered with strips of yellow, blue, and red rags, meant to represent (certainly in a very faint sense) the gorgeous hues of the east when the orb of day makes his appearance. But who shall attempt to describe the erection denominated the triumphal arch? It was a scaffolding of bamboos, resembling a gigantic gallows, and covered with streamers of the same colours as the boats, and of the same common material. Under this arch, as they called it, the whole army marched, and peals of merriment, as they did so, burst from the soldiers, it was such an absolute caricature of anything triumphal. I have no doubt but that the natives fully expected it had been originally erected in order to hang Akbar Khan upon, should we have been fortunate enough to catch him; but failing that, an attempt was made to induce them to believe it had only been erected to do honour to the victorious army. Lord Ellenborough was so anxious to shew the troops how much he estimated the successful termination of this campaign, that he must have been sadly disappointed at the manner in which the executives had burlesqued his intention. Mr. George Robins himself never could have had the conscience to call it anything but a gallows.

At Ferozepore, where we arrived on the 19th of December, I met a Prussian officer who had, I believe, been sent out by his government in order to witness the operations in Affghanistan. He seemed a very nice fellow; but as he never got farther than Ferozepore, he might as well have saved himself the trouble of travelling so far. The only operations which he had an opportunity of seeing were the balls and dinner parties given by the Governor-General and by divers regiments. However, the triumphal gallows was itself worth coming a few thousand miles to see.

While I was in Affghanistan, my friends in England had procured my removal into the 34th Regiment, which was at home. As soon, therefore, as I reached Ferozepore I purchased a palanquin, and laid a dâk to Meerut, which is nearly three hundred miles distant, and where my wife had resided during the time I was away on service. It was with heartfelt regret that I left a regiment with which I had served in so many stirring scenes, and I took leave of my companions in arms with a sad heart, having little expectation of our ever meeting again.

There is something in war which seems to bind men together. I think there is never so friendly a feeling among the members of any regiment as when on service; and, when they part after having fought in the same field, it is with a kindly disposition towards each other, totally different from that experienced on separating from common acquaintances. I dined at the mess the night before my departure, and, after a warm shake of the hand, and interchange of good wishes with each of my old comrades, I retired for a few hours' sleep to a friend's tent, from whence I set out early the next morning on my way to Meerut.

It was of the utmost consequence to me that I should proceed to England, owing to the severe calamity which had befallen me in the death of my poor father. After so many years' separation also from the rest of my family, how great was my desire again to embrace them! Yet, with the bright prospect before me of visiting home and all its attractions again, my heart yearned towards my old corps, and the brave fellows with whom I had shared so many perils.

Never was a commander more fortunate in his army than General Pollock. The behaviour of every corps comprising it was on all occasions admirable. The soldier-like and gallant bearing of the 31st, under the most trying circumstances, together with its high state of discipline, and interior economy, won the admiration of the whole force. My regret at leaving such a regiment was therefore not to be wondered at.

No sooner had I proceeded about twelve miles on my journey than it began to pour with rain, not the gentle showers that we have in England, but the water coming down in torrents. It thundered as if heaven and earth were coming together, and the forked lightning ran along the ground in every direction; altogether, I never saw a more fearful storm. The bearers could not stand under it, so they were fain to put the palanquin under the lee of a small shed, which presented itself on the road side. They huddled themselves together inside the wretched hut, through the straw roof of which the water poured down in streams. Unfortunately, the roof of my palkee was not perfectly water-proof, although I had purchased the best which was to be found in Ferozepore. The water began to ooze through, at first by the smallest drops, but as the constant stream washed away the putty, or whatever it was with which it had been caulked, it streamed through in right earnest, wetting my mattrass and every thing inside.

I could not help contrasting the progressive manner in which the element had taken possession of my stronghold, with the rise of the British power in India, At first, it was in the most humble and deferential manner that a company of speculating tradesmen obtained permission from an Indian prince to build a factory on a piece of ground allotted for the purpose. No sooner had this footing been obtained, than like the continued stream of water falling on the roof of my palkee, reinforcements and supports pressed on them from England. The head was in, and the body soon followed. Encreasing daily, at length the intruders demanded in the most haughty manner concessions from the astonished natives, the hundredth part of which would a few years before have been prayed for in the most abject manner. Following up to the letter the old proverb of " The more you get the more you may," these adventurers eventually overran the country, and their career of conquest was like the mad course of the whirlwind over the rich plains of India. Even so was it with my palanquin; for the roof at last became so completely pervious to the persevering attempts of the rain, that I ran a very good chance of being washed out of my own vehicle, when, as good luck would have it, the thick pall of heavy clouds overhead began to open, and a faint gleam of sunshine breaking forth, seemed to promise more favourable weather before long.

Having been detained by the storm for about six hours, I was anxious to proceed, and with some difficulty routing out the bearers from their shelter, I made them take up the palkee, and continued my journey. The poor wretches were half stupified by the cold and wet; and it was a perfect charity to make them trot along again. The road passes through the protected Seik states, and robberies are of frequent occurrence. In consequence of the many outrages which had at divers times been committed between Ferozepore and Loodianah, it was customary for a sowar* to attend every set of bearers, and to accompany the traveller's palanquin for the stage as an escort. After the first stage from Ferozepore, no sowar ever attended, but as I was well armed myself

* A native trooper.

I was not at all in want of their assistance. I got on well enough, until I happened during the night to fall asleep. How long I remained in this state I know not, but in the morning when I awoke, I found my palkee had been set down on the ground in the middle of a large plain, and all the bearers had absconded. I was left alone in my glory. The scoundrels were afraid to proceed during the night, and, therefore, as soon as they saw I was asleep, they had set down the palanquin, and walked off to some village in the vicinity, in order to pass the night. I shouted and swore, but all to no purpose, the only answer I got being from a pariah dog which was prowling about at some distance, and which, as soon as he heard my voice, began to bark most furiously. I could not leave my palanquin to go in search of the rascally bearers, there being little doubt that, if I did, it would be plundered in my absence. I was, therefore, fain to light a cheroot, and sat myself down on a bank to wait,

"Like Patience on a monument,"

until it should please the scoundrels to return.

About two hours after sunrise they shewed themselves at a distance, when they made a halt, and sent forward one of their number as an ambassador in order, I suppose, to see what sort of humour I was in. This worthy approached within a few yards of me, but I remarked that he kept his eye anxiously fixed on my motions, and was quite ready to make a bolt at once if I seemed likely to attempt to seize him. He held up his hands in an attitude of supplication, and told me that his comrades and himself were poor men, that they had been very much tired, and that having committed a great fault in deserting me, they were afraid to come near until assured of my forgiveness. In other words, they were fearful of getting a good thrashing all round for their rascality. I certainly would have given almost any thing to have had an opportunity of laying a stick over their backs, but I had no chance. It was evident none of them would come within reach, and running after them was out of the question; the natives being so nimble that no European would have a chance of catching them. I wanted also to get on; and, although in a furious temper, I thought it politic to assure them, that if they would come and take up the palanquin and proceed at once, I would not harm them. Seeing still a little hesitation on their parts of coming nearer until I was safely inside, I took out my double-barrelled gun, and declaring that if they attempted to bolt again I would let fly among them, I deposited myself in my vehicle, and was instantly hoisted up on their shoulders and trotted on to the next stage.

At this place was a bungalow, the only one on the road between Ferozepore and Loodianah. The bearers put down my palkee in the verandah, and before I could get out they took to their heels, and disappeared in an instant. The fact was, they were afraid of being obliged to take on the palanquin of another traveller, who was proceeding in the contrary direction to myself, and who, as he informed me, had been delayed at this place for two days, not being able to procure bearers. It is customary when palanquins meet on a journey for the bearers to change, and thus return to their own stations. The fellows who had brought me had evidently an idea that it was much easier work for them to go back empty-handed, than to carry the other traveller's palkee to their station. This would not have been allowed in lower India; but in these Seik states the authorities have no influence over the disorderly inhabitants; and, although a traveller pays for his dâk before he starts, it is seldom indeed that he finds it is regularly laid on the road, although I believe it is not usual to be quite so much troubled as I was. The postmasters at the stations send their directions to the head men of villages to lay the dâk in the same manner as in lower India, but these worthies at the villages between Ferozepore and Loodianah seldom take any notice of the matter: and I conceive there are no means of punishing them, as the country is not exactly at present under the British authority.

Fortunately, the bungalow at which I was detained was a very good one, having been built by order of Government for the accommodation of dâk travellers on this unsettled road. There was a kitmutgar,* who in a short time prepared me a capital breakfast of curried fowl and chupattees.† The gentleman who like myself was detained here, told me he had no difficulty in getting bearers until he arrived at this place, and that the

* Cook.
† Thin cakes of unleaved bread.

chokedar* of the bungalow had promised him, for a consideration, to procure bearers from a village some distance off to take him on that night. This functionary was absent on his mission when I arrived. On his return, he assured me that I had little chance of getting bearers for two days at least, but that he would do his best, and if possible I should have them by the following morning.

This was a delightful predicament to be placed in. I had been separated from my wife for a year, and had been pleasing myself with the thought, that in three days from my leaving Ferozepore, I should have the happiness of rejoining her. Not having anticipated these continued impediments, I had written from that station to inform her when I expected to reach Meerut. In addition, therefore, to the nuisance of being delayed, I knew she would be excessively anxious on finding I did not arrive, knowing that I was travelling on a very dangerous road.

My fellow-traveller and myself wandered about the whole day to beguile away the weary hours, which seemed to drag on most heavily. We

* Watchman.

threw stones at the crows which were impudently hopping about the verandah in search of the remains of our breakfasts. We then adjourned to a well which we saw at a short distance, and were amused for some time by witnessing the squabbling among a number of women who had assembled to draw water, as to who should get the first bucket. By means of these and similar diversions, we whiled away the time until the hour for tiffin, not that we were hungry, but the meal would help us to dispel the irksome moments. The old kitmutgar was a capital cook and fed us very well, so we congratulated ourselves that we were no worse off, as it was just as likely for us to have been left without bearers at a station in the middle of the jungle, where we could get nothing in the way of food or shelter. Here, at least, we had a comfortable bungalow over our heads and good living. All things have an end, and at last this long dull day came to a close. How impatiently we watched the sun descending towards the horizon: every five minutes looking out and wondering what made him move so slowly! We dined at five o'clock, and shortly afterwards my friend's new bearers made their appearance. He was anxious enough to get on, and stepping at once into his palkee, bade me farewell. I was once more alone. How I envied his luck in getting bearers, as I stood watching his palanquin receding in the distance! I was now in a more unpleasant situation than ever. I had somebody to talk to while he was delayed as well as myself; but now I could find nothing to wear away the time.

I ordered some tea to be got ready, and sitting in the verandah smoking a cheroot, while it was being prepared, I heard a continual shouting, accompanied with peals of laughter, from some persons galloping along the road towards the bungalow. The clattering of their horses' hoofs might have been heard at a great distance in the stillness of the night, had not the boisterous merriment of the riders been quite sufficient to wake up all the sleepers for miles around. While I was wondering who these noisy subjects could be, they galloped up to where I was sitting, and by the light of a cherag which I ordered to be brought, I discovered two young Seiks splendidly armed and mounted, and both as drunk as lords. They were delighted, they said, to meet a Sahib,*

* English gentleman.

as all the Feringees were such good fellows, and insisted upon singing some Seik songs to me in praise of brandy. I was excessively amused with the fellows, who were the most good natured and pleasant animals in their cups that I ever beheld. I had some rum in my palanquin, which I asked them to taste, and with which request they most willingly acquiesced. They dismounted and sat with me for three or four hours, when they told me that they were the sons of a Sirdar,* that they were going to Lahore to pay their respects to the Maharajah, Shere Sing, and that they had procured a dozen bottles of brandy from Loodianah to keep them well during the journey, as they heard it was considered a great medicine among the Feringees. They had finished eight bottles in two days, and they said they thought it was the nicest medicine they had ever tasted. It appeared they liked rum, also, for they emptied one of my bottles immediately, and wished for another; but I would not give them any more, having but one bottle left. At about eleven o'clock they prepared to depart, and with many a squeeze of the hand and expressions of friend-

* A chief.

ship, they bade me farewell and mounted their steeds. No sooner were they on the backs of their unfortunate quadrupeds, than they dashed their spurs up to the rowel heads in their flanks, and scampered off again at full speed,

"Making night hideous"

with their yells. I could hear their shouts and laughter growing fainter and fainter as they increased their distance from the bungalow, until nothing remained to disturb the silence of the night save the occasional cry of the jackall in pursuit of its prey, and the eternal chirupping of the crickets, with which every part of India teems, and which invariably keep up their monotonous concerts during the whole of the hours of darkness.

Shortly after my Seik friends had departed, I got into my palanquin and soon fell asleep. At about five o'clock in the morning, the chokedar redeemed his promise by bringing the bearers who were to take me on. Shaking my shoulder as I lay asleep, he inquired if it was my pleasure to proceed, as the cahar logue\* were ready, and

\* Palanquin bearers.

waiting. I need not say that I assured him in answer, that it most decidedly was my pleasure to proceed at once; and, rewarding the chokedar with a rupee, I ordered the bearers to take up the palanquin, and was soon again trotting along the road.

At the bungalow, I had been able to dry the mattress and other coverings of my palanquin, which had been saturated with water during the storm which I encountered when leaving Ferozepore. I had, however, caught a most severe cough and rheumatism from lying on them, and having my own clothes wet for a day and night. No sooner had I proceeded about five miles from the bungalow than the dark clouds over head began again to discharge their burdens, and showers of rain came pouring down, again wetting everything I had through and through. The roof of my palanquin was completely like a sieve, the thin lathes of wood of which it was composed, having warped from the combined effects of sun and rain, and cracked the painted canvass with which it was covered. I was not able again to dry my things, until I arrived at Meerut.

However, it was some consolation that I found bearers waiting regularly at every stage; and I proceeded on my route without stoppage all that day. Still it appeared that my journey to Meerut was ordained to be a continued chapter of accidents: for during the night the pole of my palkee broke, and down I came with a run. Happily, however, this misfortune occurred close to a native city, where I was enabled to procure a quantity of rope and a strong bamboo, by means of which, the palanquin was soon again rendered serviceable, and I continued my journey, not in the most pleasant humour in the world, as I fully expected the pole to give way again every minute.

I was agreeably disappointed. The rude splicing kept together during the whole of the next day, and that night I reached Kurnaul, where I was enabled to get a new pole to my vehicle in a very short time, there being numberless carpenters at that station, whose trade it is to make and repair palanquins. After this, I met with no more mishaps, and arrived safely at Meerut the next night, where I had been long and anxiously expected.

All the ladies of the 9th and 31st regiments, together with the depôts of invalids, women, and children were located at this station, and the next day I was quite overwhelmed with inquiries from the females on all sides regarding the health of their absent lords. As I was the first who returned from the scene of war, I had to bear the brunt of the first fire of their curiosity. They wanted to know whether this account was correct, and if that were not untrue; whether so and so did not distinguish himself particularly, and whether such a one talked constantly of his wife, and sent his love to her or not, and why he had not sent a letter by me, &c. &c.

I assured them all that their husbands were quite *au désespoir* at not being able to join them immediately, and that they all sent their love and would write by post, as they had not had time to get letters prepared when I left. I then began to make preparations for dâking down to Calcutta, which is about a thousand miles from Meerut. Being anxious to get to England as soon as possible, I had determined to travel by dâk, as the most expeditious mode.

## CHAPTER XII.

Station of Meerut—Dâk trip to Calcutta—Station of Allahabad—Benares—Beggars—The Rajmahal hills—A tiger—A wild elephant—Arrival at Calcutta—Author embarks for England—Fishing off the coast of Africa—Table Bay—Cape Town—St. Helena—A gale of wind—An Irish hooker—Kinsale—An Irish steamer—An accident—Arrival at home.

MEERUT is a very fine station, decidedly one of the best in India. The cantonments are very extensive, sufficient to accommodate six or seven thousand men, including a regiment of European cavalry, horse artillery, and infantry. Small pox is rather prevalent there, but generally the climate is not unhealthy. Shops for the sale of European wares of every description are large and numerous, and consequent on this competition the articles sold by them are at excessively moderate prices.

All the officers' bungalows have gardens attached, in which far better vegetables and fruit may be raised than those which are proffered for sale in the bazaars. Mutton, beef, fowls, &c. are plentiful, of excellent quality, and very cheap. There is capital shooting in the vicinity. Plenty of wildfowl may be had, and the station is sufficiently near to the Himalaya mountains to render it an easy matter to run up for a change of air to Simla, or some other hill station, during the hot weather. Altogether, should I ever go to India again, if I had my choice of stations, I should fix on Meerut.

The distance to Calcutta being so great, I apprehended the fatigue of the journey day and night, without halting, would be too much for my wife, while at the same time we were both anxious to accomplish it in as short a time as possible. I therefore laid a dâk first to Allahabad, which is about half way to the presidency, and from thence another to Calcutta. Four days' notice would be required by the postmaster at Allahabad to complete his arrangements, and thus we should be enabled to have a little rest on the way. It is dreadfully dull and fatiguing work to be on one's back in a close wooden box, and to be jolted day and night for ten or twelve days together. Even if the traveller is happy enough to be able to sleep during the nights, he is invariably woke up at the termination of every stage by the demand of buxees for the bearers, who have completed the distance. This is a custom which might easily be abolished, for if the men receive too little recompense for their work at the present rate, a larger sum should be charged in the first instance, instead of subjecting the traveller to the intolerable nuisance of having his slumbers broken in upon every two hours, when his rest is quite sufficiently disturbed by the incoveniences which are inseparable from this mode of travelling.

Having purchased another palanquin, with four pair of banghies,* and laid in a good stock of internal comforts in the commissariat line, the evening of the 29th of December we ensconced ourselves in our palkees, and bidding good-bye to a numer-

* Small boxes, two of which are slung on a bamboo, and carried by a bearer alongside the palanquin. These banghy burdars, as they are called, are relieved at every stage, as well as those who carry the palkee itself.

ous assembly of friends with whom we had taken a farewell dinner, we were lifted on the shoulders of our two-legged steeds, and started at the rate of about three miles and a half an hour, on our journey towards Allahabad. On the fifth day, we were set down, without accident, at the dâk bungalow at that station. The roads in this part of India are remarkably good, and it is seldom indeed that travellers meet with any delay. There are dâk bungalows at every stage, where kitmutgars are always in attendance to prepare dinner or breakfast for any traveller who may stop and require their services. A charge is made by government at each bungalow of one rupee for the use of the same, towards defraying the expenses of building and repairing these accommodations for travellers. The kitmutgar makes his own charge for the refreshments which he supplies, which, however, is generally very moderate. It must be owned that the fare is very moderate also, it being seldom the case that any thing but a curried fowl and some chupattees can be obtained. Persons accustomed to travelling, therefore, and who are fond of making themselves as comfortable as circumstances will permit, always take a private stock of cold meat, preserves, pickles, &c., by the assistance of which adjuncts to the fare procurable at the bungalow, they can at all times command a tolerable dinner. I had loaded two banghies with good things, being determined to enjoy myself as much as I could, after having been so long in Affghanistan living on the worst and scantiest food.

Immediately on arriving at Allahabad, I went to the post-master of the station, and, having ordered a dâk for Calcutta, we spent the four days which it was necessary to wait in rambling about the place. There is a fine fort at this station, comprising extensive magazines of artillery, small arms, and other munitions of war, of all descriptions. The roads about the cantonments are excessively good, and the station is altogether very pleasantly situated on the banks of the river Ganges. European troops are never stationed here, the garrison being entirely composed of sepoys. I believe the climate is tolerably healthy, and generally liked by the European residents.

On the 8th of January, our dâk arrangements having been completed, we again set forward on our journey, and proceeded without accident as far as the holy City of Benares. There we met with delay, no bearers being in waiting. After a great deal of trouble, I succeeded in hiring three sets, who agreed to take us on for thirty miles, when I was given to understand I was pretty sure to find the dâk all right. While waiting at the dâk bungalow, before I was able to conclude these arrangements, we were regularly besieged by crowds of itinerant dealers in Benares scarfs, embroidered muslins, and native paintings of great men. These fellows crowded into the compound from all sides, and it was with the greatest difficulty that I could drive them out. About fifty beggars then swarmed in, some of whom were the most disgusting objects I ever beheld. It was impossible to get rid of them by any other plan than by throwing some pice outside the compound, which had the effect of taking them away in order to scramble for the coin. Benares, being a great resort of pilgrims and of religious men, is also a favourite rendezvous for mendicants, whose constant demand of alms is very troublesome. Most of them are cripples, with frightfully distorted limbs. So fond are the natives of idleness, that parents of this sect are said to maim their offspring in infancy, that they may be objects of charity in after life, instead of having to work for their bread. At Benares, there are several native regiments, but no European soldiers.

On arriving near the Rajmahal hills, the road becomes rather dangerous, in consequence of the thick jungle which covers the country through which the Calcutta road runs, and which is infested with tigers, bears, and other beasts of prey. One evening, we halted for a couple of hours to get some tea, at a bungalow in the centre of a dense forest. The chokedar informed me that a tiger was in the nightly habit of going his rounds close to the house, which they were in consequence obliged to keep carefully shut up after dark. He pointed out a tree close by, from under which a native had been carried off by the monster the evening before we arrived. The poor wretch's blood was still fresh in gouts upon the grass at the spot where he had been seized.

The chokedar also showed me some places at which the bears were in the nightly habit of digging for roots, within forty yards of the house. One of these animals had killed a woman who had been gathering sticks in the forest, a few days before our arrival.

It was night when we left this centrical spot of agreeable society; and I remarked, as we proceded along the road, which was overhung with thick jungle, that the bearers kept very close together, looking fearfully round on every side, while the mussalchees* poured a constant and plentiful supply of oil upon their torches, which they flourished high over their heads, in order to keep off any of the savage inhabitants of the wilderness that might be partial to black men.

It is singular that a tiger invariably seizes the last man of any party on which he may make an attack. The natives are perfectly aware of this fact, and I could hardly help laughing at the anxiety each bearer shewed to keep in front. The noise of the bearers, and the flaming light of the torches generally keep off the wild denizens of the forest from a dâk party; but the poor fellows who carry the letters for the postmasters, and who are always alone, are very frequently taken away. Some years ago, a wild elephant took possession of

* Torch bearers.

a part of the road to the upper provinces, and completely stopped the post by killing every person who came by. The cause of the stoppage being at length discovered, a party of officers went out, and shot the gigantic brute.

We were lucky enough to meet with no molestation from the tigers, and proceeded without further delay on our journey until we arrived at Augurporah, which is about nine miles from Calcutta, and where we did not find any bearers waiting for us. It was very annoying to be impeded just at the termination of our travels, but fortunately I discovered that there were some stables at this place, belonging to Mr. Cook, the livery-stable keeper of Calcutta, and I was able to hire a buggy and horse, while the man who superintended the concern undertook to take charge of my palanquin and banghies until the bearers should arrive, when they were to bring them on to the hotel at which I purposed staying. We arrived at Calcutta in this vehicle, on the evening of the 15th of January, heartily tired of dâk travelling, and thanking our stars that we had no more of it in anticipation. But still the horribly dull and long sea-voyage stared me in the face, before I could once again set foot upon my native soil.

I obtained a passage in the first ship that sailed, and embarked, on the 29th of January, from Cooly Bazaar. No sooner had we taken possession of our cabin than the anchor was hove up, and we began to drop down the river. As the gallant vessel laid over to the breeze, and her broad canvass bellied with the wind, urging her forward like some vast monster through the waves, how delightful was the thought, that at length we were really on our way home, and that the land of pestilence and death in which I had so long sojourned was fast receding from our view!

A ship is the most uncomfortable abode in the world at any time, but more particularly while the pilot is on board at the commencement of a voyage. Right glad, therefore, was I when I saw him take his departure, on arriving at the sand heads. While the pilot is on board a ship, nothing is in order;— every thing is at sixes-and-sevens. No sooner, however, has the vessel got into deep water, and is again under the control of her legitimate commander, than things bear a totally different aspect. Neatness and regularity then take the place of disorder and confusion, and the situation of the passengers, accordingly, becomes more tolerable.

We had a very fine passage to the Cape of Good Hope, not having experienced any bad weather until our arrival near the coast of Africa. But our voyage was tedious, in consequence of the ship being very heavily laden, and a sluggish sailer.

When about a hundred miles from the coast, we had a gale of wind, but not very severe. After it had subsided, the master determined to put into the Cape for fresh provisions and water, our stock having nearly run out. When sounding on our arriving near the coast, the sailors fastened hooks to the lead, and pulled up very fine fish at every heave. One evening, we ran very near in shore at Cape Agullas, and every man on board throwing out a line, it was amusing to see how fast we pulled up the fish. Some of them weighed from forty to fifty pounds, and were of most excellent flavour. Our tackle consisted of large hooks baited with pieces of salt pork, and fastened to a strong line, with a weight attached to sink it to the bottom. It was no sooner there than the fish bit most ravenously, and I am sure that in a day we might have caught enough to freight the ship.

The number of gannets, cormorants, and seagulls which frequent the entrance to Table Bay is astonishing. We were becalmed when but a few miles from the shore, and had capital sport, firing at them with ball, as they heavily flapped their huge wings in the air, or idly reposed on the calm bosom of the placid sea. At last, a breeze sprang up, and we were able to make our way in. We were quickly surrounded by boats from the shore, and no sooner was the anchor dropped than I stepped into one of them, delighted enough at the idea of once again standing on *terra firma*, after having been for upwards of two months cooped up in a floating prison.

Cape Town reminded me much of the towns in Germany, the houses and shops being built exactly on the same plan. The place itself is not large, but the houses appear to be comfortable and well-built, and the shops are plentifully supplied with every article of consumption. It is altogether a very nice station for troops, the climate being exceedingly fine : fish, flesh, and fowl are remarkably good and cheap, and first-rate shooting is to be had in the vicinity.

On the second day after our arrival, a mass of

dark thick clouds was seen overhanging the summit of Table Mountain, foreboding by their presence that a storm was gathering. The master of our ship was very anxious to get on board and put to sea, Table Bay being a very dangerous harbour for a vessel to ride out a gale in. His engagements on shore, however, prevented our embarking until late at night, when the gale had already commenced. On arriving at the pier, the scene was very grand. The waves were running mountains high, and the ships at anchor were tossing up and down, like so many cockle-shells. Their tall masts, seen in bold relief by the lightning that blazed around, seemed as if they would pierce the thick canopy of lowering clouds which hung in dense masses above them. Crowds of spectators thronged the pier to see us off. It was with the greatest difficulty that we got into the boat which was to convey us to the ship, the sailors being obliged to keep her some distance from the piles, to prevent her being dashed to pieces against them by the sea. At last, we all got safely in, and away we went with a closely reefed sail, our frail bark riding like a sea-bird over the boiling waters.

We soon reached the ship, and the anchor being quickly hove up, we stood out to sea before the gale, and long before morning the coast of Africa had faded from our view. The wind continued fair, and in fourteen days we passed St. Helena, that barren rock which was at once the prison and the tomb of the mightiest spirit of the age in which he lived. How truly do the words of our immortal poet apply to the sad fate of the Great Napoleon!

> Ill weav'd ambition, how much art thou shrunk!
> When that this body did contain a spirit,
> A kingdom for it was too small a bound;
> But now two paces of the vilest earth
> Is room enough.

We passed the island with a spanking breeze, and in a few days made Ascension, of turtle notoriety. From the view which I had of this place I should say it was only fit for turtle to live on. Its aspect from the sea is most barren and desolate. The voyage now became indescribably irksome. Every day seemed a year in its tedious course. But this is always the case with a long sea trip. At first, the novelty of the situation, and the knowledge that the voyage is all before one, prevent that anxiety for its termination which towards the close of it is so insupportable. The last month appears as long as the three preceding ones.

At length, we made the western islands, and, as I believe is generally the case in that part of the world, it blew a regular gale of wind. Fortunately it was fair, and we ran before it at the rate of ten knots an hour, the vast billows which followed our wake seeming every moment ready to swallow us up, while showers of spray flew over the forecastle and deck, as the vessel dashed through the blue waters. The wind whistled hoarsely through the cordage, and the ship creaked and groaned in her mad course as the gale increased, and bowed the tall masts before it like willow wands. The master determined to carry on all the sail he could, never himself leaving the deck; and, at last, as the wind blew stronger and stronger, we absolutely flew through the waves. Nothing is so inspiriting as a fair breeze at sea, no matter how much of it, so long as it is in the right quarter, and sail can be carried. We rubbed our hands and chuckled with glee as we speculated on the probability of reaching England in a week, if the wind held fair.

Bets were made as to the day on which we should take the pilot on board, &c. &c. There was now no doubt but that our long dull voyage was at last very near its termination, and that in a few more days we should once again be gladdened with the sight of the white cliffs of our own sea-girt home.

When about fifty miles from the coast of Ireland, we fell in with a hooker belonging to Kinsale, which had been blown out to sea in a gale of wind. The crew soon came alongside, and, fastening their boat to our ship, a regular barter took place between the sailors and themselves. They supplied our men with bread and potatoes, in exchange for straw hats, shirts, and old clothes of every description. Towards evening, they began to make preparations for their departure; and, as I was quite tired of the ship, and longed most ardently to get on dry land as soon as possible, I made a bargain with them to take myself and wife, with a servant and our baggage, to Kinsale, whence I purposed proceeding to Cork, and crossing over to Bristol in a steamer.

The sea was rather high, and it was not very easy to get into the boat, which it was necessary to keep a short distance from the ship, in order to prevent her being swamped. Sailors, however, are fertile in inventions, and a machine was soon rigged up to transport us from one craft to the other. An arm-chair was slung through a block at the yard-arm, and a rope, attached to the bottom of the seat, was thrown to the crew of the hooker, who, by its means, were enabled to guide the chair to their boat, keeping it tolerably steady on the way as soon as it was hoisted a sufficient height from the deck of the ship.

The tackle altogether was very ingenious; but at the same time the transit from one vessel to the other in it was rather a ticklish affair. Fortunately, Mrs. Greenwood was blessed with pretty strong nerves; so much so, that she never troubled any one else with her fears, however hazardous the situations in which she might be placed. I seated myself first in the chair, and was soon on board the hooker. The abyss of roaring sea that intervened between the craft, and which appeared very broad when one was suspended in mid air above it, was, however, rather a fearful sight, and I felt anxious while my wife was undergoing the passage. But it was very well managed, and she was hauled on board the hooker without accident. The servant and baggage having followed, we were cast off, and proceeded on our course, being about forty miles distant from our port.

The hooker was an open boat used for fishing, and having a crew of six sturdy Paddys. The spray flew fast and thick over us as she stood towards the land against a rough head sea, and I was fain to get my wife under cover in a small place resembling a dog kennel, which was built under the bowsprit, and into which it was necessary to crawl on all fours. Inside, there was room enough to lie down, but not to sit upright. In it were kept all the stores of the boat, including a vast quantity of potatoes. Over these some straw had been laid, on which the fishermen had arranged our bedding which we had brought from the ship; and, with the natural kindness of their countrymen, they made most anxious inquiries as to whether the "misthress" was comfortable, very frequently, after she had managed to creep in.

As the night advanced, we began to get very hungry, not having had time to eat any dinner on board the ship during the bustle of packing up our things and departing. No sooner had I mentioned this fact, than the crew of the hooker immediately putting a large iron pot on the fire, that burned in the centre of the boat, and round which they were huddled, the night being very cold, commenced boiling some potatoes for us. They had also a mackarel on board, which they had caught some days before and salted. This was likewise put on the fire, and in a short time every thing being ready, we had a fine feast on these homely viands. Plates, knives or forks, they had none, and probably knew not the use of such things. We had, therefore, to use our fingers, which the old proverb says, were made before spoons; and I must say that I never enjoyed a supper more in my life. The potatoes were beautiful and capitally boiled, the kind and hearty welcome of these poor Irishmen being sufficient of itself to have made even homelier food palatable.

The solicitude which they displayed in providing for our wants, and pressing us to eat more of the food which, I dare say, was often scarce enough among them, went home to the heart. I had often heard of the hospitality and kind-heartedness of the lower order of Irish, and it was gratifying in the extreme to see these virtues so fully exemplified on the first occasion on which I had come into contact with them.

These men had all taken the temperance pledge; and I, for one, can bear witness how much they respected it. The night was bitterly cold, and a sharp driving sleet which flew thickly upon the fishermen who had no cover from it, must have rendered their situation one of extreme hardship. I had brought a couple of bottles of brandy with me from the ship, and I offered it to them in order to keep the cold out. To my utter surprise, they resolutely declined touching it, saying that they had taken the vow, and never tasted spirits by any chance. I was much astonished at their steady refusal, and, had I not myself witnessed this fact, I should have been unwilling to believe it, knowing from my experience of the army, where three-fifths or more of the soldiers are from the sister isle, that drink is the Irishman's curse, and the one which he finds it most difficult to resist. In my own regiment I have seen many, many soldiers, superior men in every way, who had no fault but a taste for the bottle, and whom that one unfortunate failing always prevented from filling any situation of trust. Common soldiers they remained, or if promoted, were broken again almost immediately.

The next day, we got into the harbour of Kinsale, and I was much struck by the beauty of the view at the entrance. The scenery is most enchanting, and quite rivals that of the Cove of Cork. We lost no time in landing, and, after having passed our things through the custom house, sat down to a most plentiful breakfast at one of the nicest little hotels I ever entered. I gave all my bedding, blankets, and cabin furniture which I had brought from the ship, to the fishermen, who had behaved so well to us; and, in addition, gave them a *carte blanche* to enjoy all the good things in the larder of the hotel, a privilege of which they availed themselves to a surprising extent. By the enormous quantity of provisions which they demolished, they gave evident tokens of having highly approved of the quality of mine host's fare.

Kinsale is a remarkably pretty town, delightfully situated, about nine miles from Cork. Had I a few months to spare, I do not know any place which I would sooner revisit. I regretted, while there, that I was obliged to depart so soon, but finding that a steamer was to leave Cork the same day on which I landed, it was necessary to quit without delay.

Accordingly, I hired two jaunting cars, on one of which, I packed my baggage, and the other was occupied by Mrs. Greenwood and myself. Our charioteers smacked their whips and rattled away in first-rate style, being, doubtless, stimulated in their exertions by floating visions of certain measures of whisky, with which I had promised to reward them, in case they should arrive in time for us to secure a passage in the steam boat.

The scenery of the road between Kinsale and Cork is remarkably picturesque and beautiful, and well worth a visit to Ireland. We had no time to lose in admiring it, or I should decidedly have spent some hours on the way. We arrived at Cork just as the steamer was about to start, and were thus fortunate enough to save our passage, which, had we been a minute later, would have been lost.

Those who have never been in Ireland, and who are fond of fine scenery, I recommend to go to Bristol, and, taking the steamer thence to Cork, they will be delighted by a series of beautiful little views, which I do not believe to be equalled anywhere. I have travelled over a great part of the globe myself, but in the matter of scenery, I never was so much gratified as on this, my first visit, to the emerald isle.

The accommodation on board was tolerable, and we had a good many fellow-passengers in the saloon. Vast quantities of pigs filled up the main deck, while the fore part of the vessel was crowded with some as rich specimens of the lower order of Irish as were ever imported. What they could be going to England for, I could not imagine; but a merrier set of fellows I never beheld. I am sure that the most conscientious Jew who ever cried " auld clowsh !" would not have given five shillings for the whole wardrobe of these "*pisantry ;*" yet they were all in the best humour, and in as high spirits as if they were

Monarchs of all they surveyed;

instead, poor wretches, of being in want of the common necessaries of life !

A great annoyance on board the steam-boat which, I believe, is common to all those craft from Ireland, was a marvellous ill savour from the swine with which the deck was lumbered. It penetrated every part of the vessel, and I was surprised that such a nuisance should exist on board passage boats of this class. Most people are sick enough at sea, without such an adjunct to their delights as the odour of a pig-stye.

Until we arrived within a few miles of our destination, the excursion was pleasant enough. All the passengers were collected on deck, admiring the scenery, and discussing the merits of the various hotels at Bristol, when suddenly a violent explosion, succeeded by eight or ten others in rapid succession, struck a panic among them. A vast column of steam rose from the hatchways, followed by a rush of the "pisantry" from the fore part of the vessel, where the boiling water was flying about in all directions. Such a scene of confusion I never beheld—women shrieking, some on their knees crossing and blessing themselves, the men swearing, and the porkers squeaking in most inharmonious medley. It was very evident that the boiler had burst and injured the vessel considerably, as she immediately heeled over on one side; and, had not three steamers at once arrived to her assistance, I have no doubt but that she would have gone down. One of the assisting boats was made fast on each side of our disabled craft, while the other took her in tow, in which condition we made our way to Bristol.

Providential, indeed, was it for us that the accident did not occur in the open sea, where assistance could not have been procured! As it was, the only passengers that suffered any inconvenience, were our friends the pigs, some twenty or thirty of which had been scalded to death when the explosion took place.

We arrived at Bristol about nine o'clock at night, and, after having taken some tea at an hotel there, we ensconced ourselves in the twelve o'clock night train for London. I had never seen a railway before, and the velocity of the travelling, together with the easiness of the carriages surprised me much. I could not help contrasting in my own mind the difference between the English mode of getting over the ground and the Indian dâk, by which I had travelled so many hundred miles during my journey homeward. We reached London in four hours; and, taking a cab, in a very short time we were set down before my mother's house.

How well I had remembered its aspect, since I left it to commence my career in India! I paused for a moment before I knocked for admittance, and could hardly persuade myself that nearly eight years had really passed away since I saw it last, while the events and scenes which I had gone through seemed to float before me like a vision of the night. Outside the house every thing appeared exactly the same as on the day of my departure, and yet within, alas, how many changes had taken place! The delight which overflowed my heart at the idea of again embracing the survivors of my family was checked by the sad thoughts of those who were laid low in the cold grave!

At the early hour of the morning at which we arrived, the servants were all in bed, and I had to make a pretty continued noise at the door before we could obtain admittance. At last, we got in, and, rushing up stairs to my mother's room, in a moment I was encircled in her arms.

\* \* \* \* \* \*

The first piece of intelligence that I heard was, that I was still in the 31st regiment. I had written from India to my mother on the first receipt of the news of her having obtained an exchange for me into the 34th, acquainting her that I did not like it at all, having no wish to leave the corps with which I had served in many eventful scenes. No sooner did my letter arrive, than she forwarded it to the Horse Guards, and the Commander in Chief, on the circumstances being explained to him, was kind enough to cancel the appointment, leaving me in my old place.

## CHAPTER XIII.

### SUPPLEMENTARY.

Remarks on India—The Indian army—Native regiments—Singular feat—Lieutenant Mayne—Horse artillery—Captain Abbot's troop—Foot artillery—Costume and pay—Penurious system—The Sepoys—Local Corps—Officer's pensions—Pay of officers—A subaltern's expenses—" Boat allowance"—Troops in the Presidencies—Anglo-Indian Army—The Seiks—The Zemindars—Affairs of the Punjab—Hopes for the future.

A FEW years ago, little curiosity existed among the generality of people in England, respecting the affairs of the Indian empire, unless they happened to be connected in business with traders there. Even when families had members of their own blood in the service of the East India Company, they hardly knew what situations they filled, or what duties they performed, but supposed that their chief employments in India were riding in a palanquin, eating curry, and smoking a hookah.

Since my return to England, I have met with many people who have been most anxious to gain information as to the resources and military powers of the British in India, and I have, therefore, given a sketch of the different branches of the Anglo-Indian army, describing their various customs and avocations, their mode of living, their pay, and other particulars. I have done this in the form of a supplement, that those of my readers who care not for such things, may have a fair excuse for leaving unread that which does not interest them.

The European portion of the Company's army is composed of horse artillery, foot artillery, and infantry. Of these corps, those of the horse artillery consist of the finest-looking men. To account for this, I have heard that the first pick of the recruits who are sent out on the Company's establishment falls to the share of this branch of the service. The foot artillery have the next choice, and the regiments of infantry the last. In Bengal, there are nine troops of horse artillery, five battalions of foot artillery of five companies each; one corps of engineers, two regiments of infantry, and one of sappers and miners, which compose the whole of the European force in the service of the Company in that presidency. There are, in addition to the Europeans, four troops of Native horse artillery and two battalions of Native foot artillery, of ten companies each.

The bulk of the force is composed of natives. Of these there are eleven regiments of regular cavalry, seventy-four regiments of infantry of the line, with eight corps of irregular horse, and various contingents and local corps. The regiments of regular cavalry are very fine looking men, and well mounted; but I do not think them equal to the irregulars. The regular troops are armed like our dragoons, and have saddles and bridles of the English pattern which, I think, renders them much less effective than they would be if they were furnished with their own national weapons, (in which they have more confidence) and if they had their horses caparisoned in the Hindostanee manner. The irregular cavalry are all mounted and armed in the native fashion, and some of the feats which these wild riders perform are very extraordinary.

They will gallop on horse-back, at full speed,

past a bottle placed on the ground at a considerable distance from them, and then throwing the reins on their chargers' neck, will turn round and fire their long matchlocks at the bottle, and often break it with a single ball. Another singular feat which they are in the habit of performing, is to take up a tent peg, driven deep into the earth, on the point of a spear. The horseman at a given signal, lays his spear in rest, charges in full career at the tent peg; and, burying the point in the wood, it is seldom that he will fail to get it out of the ground, and take it away upon his lance. They can throw themselves under their horses' bellies, or hang down on one side by the mane, and perform a great variety of feats of the same kind, while their steeds are going at full speed. Many of them galloping past a brass lotah,* will throw themselves out of their saddles; and, hanging by one hand on their horse's neck, with a single stroke of their tulwar† in the

* Vessels which are used by the natives when drinking water.

† A native sword. Those weapons used by the irregulars are generally of exquisite temper, and are highly valued by them, having perhaps been in their families for several generations.

other, will cut the vessel in two pieces, and swing themselves into their seats again, without checking their charger's speed.

On the slippery English saddle, it would be impossible for these men to perform tricks of the kind; but those they use being covered with a number of cloths put on in a peculiar manner, it would be difficult for them to be thrown out of their seats, while the bits which they employ are so severe, that they can stop their horses short when going at full speed with the greatest ease.

These irregular corps form a totally distinct branch of the service from the regular cavalry, being often commanded by infantry officers. When they like their commanders, they will attempt any enterprize, however desperate. There was an officer in the Jellalabad garrison, who made himself very conspicuous in many most daring and desperate attacks on the enemy when they were in immeasurably superior force, during the time that Sir Robert Sale and his gallant band were besieged by Akbar Khan. This gentleman was Lieutenant Mayne; he belonged, I believe, to a regiment of native infantry, but held the command of some irregular cavalry. He was an excellent horseman, and commonly rode a large powerful pale-coloured steed, on which he had led so many daring charges, and cut down so many of the enemy with his own hand, that he was known by the *soubriquet* of "Death on the pale horse." Sure enough, wherever the pale horse was seen, numbers of the enemy quickly bit the dust. I heard that the Affghans knew him so well at last, that no matter what their superiority of force might be if they caught sight of Mayne on his conspicuous charger, they would go to the right-about at once, and never risk an encounter, if there was a chance of getting away.

The European horse artillery are splendid-looking troops, and the officers a very superior set of men, who know their duty thoroughly. Their practice is excellent, and I do not think it could be surpassed anywhere. On service, however, there is a great fault with the Bengal horse artillery. The men, who are of the largest size and of great weight, even without their heavy accoutrements, ride on all the horses which are harnessed in the guns. This is decidedly bad. In the first place, the horses bred in Hindostan are not powerful enough to drag the cannon with such heavy weights on their backs; and, secondly, it is impossible for each pair of horses to act simultaneously with different hands guiding them, when urging them to any particularly strenuous exertion, in consequence of the guns sticking fast in hollows, or among rocks. The system in the Bombay service is much better; with their guns, there are light men who ride the near horse of each pair, and drive the other in precisely the same way as a postilion drives a post-chaise. The consequence is, that the Bombay guns will go up hills and through difficult places unassisted, while those of Bengal could not move through without having strong fatigue-parties from the infantry to drag them along. This advantage, however, I believe to be the only one which the Bombay artillery has over that of Bengal.

The most effective troop which we had with us in Affghanistan was that commanded by Captain Abbot, which was equipped on a system of his own. He had Affghan horses, which are accustomed to privations of every kind from their being colts; and these were ridden by light natives, so that the greater part of their strength was husbanded for the work of dragging the cannon. Instead of carrying his shot and ammunition on heavy tumbrils, which were the most unwieldly and troublesome things imaginable, frequently delaying us hours and hours while they were being drawn up the steep ascents by the soldiers, Captain Abbot had all his stores carried in small boxes, slung in pairs on the backs of horses on pack-saddles, and seated above them on each horse, a gunner who, being of light weight, did not with the addition of the shot boxes make a load which the animal was not perfectly able to carry. The consequence was, that this troop would go full gallop up hills without fatigue-parties at all from the infantry, where it required many hours of painful toil to drag up the other guns.

The guns of the foot artillery are most of them drawn up by bullocks, which have a most grotesque look, and I believe they are very much objected to by the officers, many of whom I have heard complain most sadly of them. In other respects, nothing could surpass the efficiency of the Company's foot artillery. They are constantly exercised, and their practice is not to be surpassed. I should imagine that they will be provided with horses before long, instead of the bullocks which they now have, and which are not only very liable to get footsore on a long march, but from their obstinacy are difficult to manage. I much wonder that the government have continued using them so long, and can only account for it on the score of a misjudged economy.

The European regiments of infantry are armed, accoutred, and disciplined in a precisely similar manner to those of the royal army, from which it would be difficult to distinguish them. They have invariably upheld the character of British soldiers whenever they have been on service, and on several occasions have greatly signalized themselves.

The native regiments of the line are dressed as nearly as possible like the Europeans, but wear no leather peaks in front of their chacos, it being I believe against their caste to do so; and, instead of leather stocks about their necks, they wear a small band of cowries.* The native officers are distinguished by having strings of large gold beads, instead of the cowries. The sepoys, as the privates are called, are recruited from the

* Small white shells.

best class of natives, no man of inferior caste being admitted. In some corps, they have very fine-looking men, many of them measuring six feet three or four inches in height. The pay of a sepoy is seven rupees a month. This allowance is increased after long service, and they get something extra when on the march. In India, where the rate of wages is very low, this pay is considered handsome, and consequently the very best castes of men offer themselves as recruits to the Company's army. There is one custom in the native regiments which I have heard much disapproved of by the officers. It is the promotion of men by seniority to the non-commissioned ranks, and not by merit. The consequence is, that the men holding the higher ranks of native officers are so old as to be of little use. With us it is different: merit is the test of promotion in the non-commissioned ranks and not length of service; by which means a spirit of emulation is raised in the breast of the young soldier, which would not exist if he felt that he could only rise in his profession as his hair grew gray.

There is another penurious system of the

Indian government which is a great drawback to the efficiency of the native infantry. They have not half so many European officers attached to each regiment as they ought to have; and even of the small number which are the Company's regulation, the greater part are absent from their corps holding staff situations, while it is no uncommon thing for a young ensign of a couple of years' service to have the command of two companies of his regiment, and be the only European officer with them. How is it possible that the youth, however well intentioned, should understand and enter into the various feelings and prejudices, which are so many and peculiar among the native soldiery; or how inspire them with that sentiment of devotion to himself which is so necessary? The sepoy looks up to an officer who understands him with feelings of absolute veneration; and numberless instances are on record of his having laid down his life without regret to save a superior who had gained his affection, or failing in that, has died with him.

The sepoys do not live in barracks as the European soldiers, nor have they any habitation found

## THE SEPOYS. 349

them by government. They build villages of huts at each station to which they are sent, in which they live with their families, while their arms and accoutrements are kept in small houses of puckah* work, which are erected by the Company. A line of these bells of arms is to be seen on each sepoy parade ground, while the arms of the European soldiers are kept in racks in their barracks. Neither do the sepoys ever wear their uniform, excepting when on duty. They always appear, save on those occasions, in their own costume, but are easily distinguished from the other natives by their superior size, cleanliness and soldier-like deportment. I believe it would be against their caste to cook their dinners with their uniforms on; and, in consequence of this prejudice, which they would rather die than violate, many of the sepoys belonging to the regiments which accompanied us to Cabul, not having time to take their clothes off on the road in order to prepare their food, eat nothing for upwards of a fortnight but parched gram,† a quantity of which they had provided at Jellalabad for the purpose.

\* Brick.  † A kind of pea.

If suddenly required, I should think that these seventy-four regiments of Bengal native infantry could each bring, on an average, about seven hundred effective bayonets into the field, making due allowance for sick, &c., &c. In addition to this large force of infantry in Bengal, there are the following local corps, which, I believe, are most of them equal to the regular regiments :—

The Calcutta native militia.
The Ramghur light infantry battalion.
The Hill Rangers.
The Nusseeree battalion.
The Sermoar battalion.
The Kemaoon battalion.
The Assam light infantry.
The Mhairwarrah local battalion.
The Sylhet light infantry battalion.
1st. Assam Sebundy corps.
2nd. Assam Sebundy corps.
The Hurrianah light infantry battalion.
The Nimaur Bheel corps.
The Malwah Bheel corps.
Several military police battalions.
European invalid veteran company.

1st. Oude local infantry.
2nd Oude local infantry.
The Jaudpore legion.
The Bundlekund legion.


In Bengal, there is also at present a large and very effective force of the royal army. It is composed of the following corps :—

H.M. 3rd. light dragoons.
H.M. 16th. lancers.
H.M. 3rd. regiment of foot.
H.M. 9th. regiment of foot.
H.M. 10th. do.
H.M. 29th. do.
H.M. 31st. do.
H.M. 39th. do.
H.M. 40th. do.
H.M. 50th. do.
H.M. 62nd. do.


The officers of the Company's army do not purchase their commissions as is the case in the royal service, but rise progressively by seniority.

After twenty years' service, they are entitled to retire on the full pay of the rank they hold, if above that of Captain. Should they unluckily be still subalterns, after so long a service, they are nevertheless entitled to a Captain's pension, which is a very considerate arrangement of the Court of Directors, as their officers services would be very badly requited if government gave them a less pension than that of a Captain. The pay of an ensign on full batta and tentage is two hundred and two rupees a month; that of a lieutenant is two hundred and fifty-six rupees; a captain's four hundred and sixty, including the contingent allowance of fifty rupees for a company. A major receives seven hundred, and a lieutenant-colonel between fourteen and fifteen hundred, including four hundred rupees command allowance.

The officers of the royal army receive the same pay while in India as those of the Company's service; and a man of tolerable prudence may always make shift to live on it, although as a subaltern it is rather pinching work, the expenses which must be incurred being so much more than they are in any other country. The great number of servants which it is necessary to keep constitute a large item in the monthly expenses, which are for a subaltern's establishment on a moderate scale, as follow:—

| | |
|---|---|
| Messing and wine bill | 60 Rs. |
| Share of bungalow rent, (supposing two officers live together) | 25 ,, |
| Kitmutgar, table attendant | 8 ,, |
| Mussalchee, torch bearer and scullion | 4 ,, |
| Sirdar bearer, house attendant | 6 ,, |
| Chokedar, or watchman | 4 ,, |
| Bheesty, or water-carrier | 4 ,, |
| Dhobee, or washerman | 6 ,, |
| Syce, or groom | 6 ,, |
| Two grasscutters | 8 ,, |
| Mahter, or scavenger | 4 ,, |
| Classie, or tent-pitcher | 6 ,, |
| During eight months in the year, four coolies for pulling the punkah and watering tatties* | 16 ,, |
| Total | 157 Rs. |

\* Frames made of a kind of grass, which being fitted into the doors of a bungalow during the prevalence of the hot winds are kept constantly wet, by coolies employed for the purpose, and which have the effect of cooling the hot air that passes through them into the house.

This scale of expenditure, which, be it observed, is a very moderate one, will, therefore, leave an ensign an overplus of a few rupees a month, which it may be presumed will, with strict economy, be enough to feed his horse, pay for his clothes, and other incidental expenses. When the lieutenantcy is obtained, the extra fifty rupees a month that are added to his pay, will give the young officer the means of much increasing his amusements and comforts. It is very hard work for an ensign to make both ends meet; but a lieutenant can manage very well.

When a young officer arrives for the first time in India, he is allowed a sum of money by Government, which is termed "boat allowance," to pay his expenses on the way to join his regiment, if up the country, the usual means of doing which is by water. This, however, is barely enough for the purpose, and he cannot fit himself out with a good horse, a tent, and other necessaries, for less than one hundred pounds. This sum he should have in his pocket when commencing his career in India, in order to keep clear from debt, which is the ruin of many promising young men, who, once in the clutches of the money-lending bloodsuckers with whom the East abounds, are never again able to extricate themselves from their difficulties.

In addition to the large force in the service of the East India Company in Bengal, there are also a great number of troops in the presidencies of Bombay and Madras. They are as follow :—

### BOMBAY PRESIDENCY.

#### ROYAL ARMY.

H.M. 14th. light dragoons.
H.M. 2nd. regiment of foot.
H.M. 13th. do.
H.M. 17th. do.
H.M. 22nd. do.
H.M. 28th. do.
H.M. 78th. do.
H.M. 86th. do.

#### COMPANY'S TROOPS.

One brigade of European horse artillery.
Two battalions of European foot artillery.
One native do.
Engineers.
Three regiments of native regular cavalry.
Two regiments of European infantry.

Twenty-six regiments of native infantry.
Marine battalion.
Three regiments of irregular cavalry.
And some local corps.

## MADRAS.

### ROYAL ARMY.

H.M. 15th. hussars.
H.M. 4th. regiment of foot.
H.M. 21st. fusileers.
H.M. 25th. regiment.
H.M. 57th. do.
H.M. 63rd. do.
H.M. 84th. do.
H.M. 94th. do.

### COMPANY'S TROOPS.

One corps horse artillery.
Four battalions of European foot artillery.
1 company gun lascars.
Engineers.
Sappers and miners.
Two regiments of European infantry.
Eight regiments of native cavalry.
Fifty-two regiments of native infantry.
Two companies of European veterans.
Two battalions of native veterans.

Few persons in England with whom I have ever conversed on Indian affairs have had the slightest idea that the Anglo-Indian army was on so large a scale. Surprising, indeed, is it, and well may surrounding nations admire the commercial prosperity of England when it is remembered that this vast force of well-disciplined and hardy troops is kept up entirely by a company of merchants who, by their means, have obtained possession of so extensive and valuable an empire in the East! The dominion over which the East India Company holds sway, is indeed great; but, to secure our peaceable possession of it, we must have more. We must never stand still in India. Our only plan is to advance, but not to such countries as Affghanistan, so remote and so worthless.

The rich plains of the Punjab, irrigated as they are by five rivers, that fatten the fertile soil with their waters, while they afford easy means of transport, are a prize worth grasping at. Should the British take possession of the government which the Seiks are unworthy and unable to hold, the native population would be benefited beyond measure. The Punjabees are on all occasions tyrannized over by their insolent and overbearing masters, and the fact of a man's accumulating wealth by means of his honest industry is enough to seal his fate. The avaricious Seiks are sure to lay hold of some pretext, however unjust, in order to plunder him of his riches, nor is it improbable that his life may be sacrificed to their rapacity.

The advance of British troops across the Sutledge would be hailed with delight by the poor wretches who are groaning under the yoke of the Seik invaders. These rulers have no more right to the country than we have, theirs being only that of conquest which, of course, holds good no longer than they are able to sustain it by the sword.

Whilst I was marching through the country, on the return of the army from Cabul, I had many conversations with the Zemindars and influential people who inhabited the villages that lay in our route. In that part of the Punjab which lies between the Jhelum and Peshawur, these people were particularly hostile towards the Seiks, and their invariable question to us, after the first salutation, was, "When are you going to invade the Punjab, now that the Cabul campaign is brought to a satisfactory conclusion?" They added, that no sooner should a British force cross the Sutledge *en route* to Lahore, than all the inhabitants of the north would rise *en masse* against the Seiks; that they could easily master them, the Fort of Attok, and a few other fortresses being all the hold which they had over the country; and that the spirit of the inhabitants being most hostile to them, they would cut off their provisions, if they could not overcome them in the field.

There is another powerful inducement for us to take possession of the Punjab, in addition to the value of the territory itself. It is the wonderful moral effect which our beating the Seiks would have upon the inhabitants of India generally, both our own subjects and those of independent princes. The natives themselves have prodigious ideas of the power of the Seiks, and are inclined to believe that, in the event of a struggle, they would be successful. The prosperous termination, therefore, of a war with the masters of the Punjab, of which there could be no doubt, would have the effect of convincing them, that, the British being really invincible, it would be useless for any nation, however powerful and warlike, to risk a contest, since it would surely end in their being obliged to succumb to our superior prowess.

It is fortunate that at this crisis of affairs in India, the helm of government is held by so able a hand. Under Lord Ellenborough's firm and clear-sighted rule, we shall hear of no such exhibitions of folly and disaster as unfortunately took place in Affghanistan. His government commenced with a career of victory which has been ominous of future glory to the British name. He has the thorough confidence of the troops, who well know that when the right moment arrives, he will open new scenes of honour and conquest to them; and I doubt not, that the hour is at hand when the British standard will float triumphant at Lahore, and when to our late victories in Affghanistan, Scinde, and China, will be added the profitable conquest of the Punjab.

THE END.

LONDON:
Printed by Schulze and Co., 13, Poland Street.

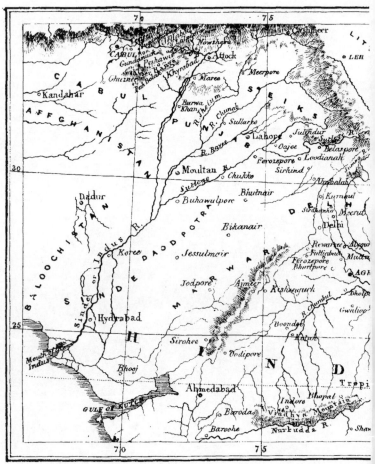

Published by H. Colburn 13 Gt Marlborough St. 1844.

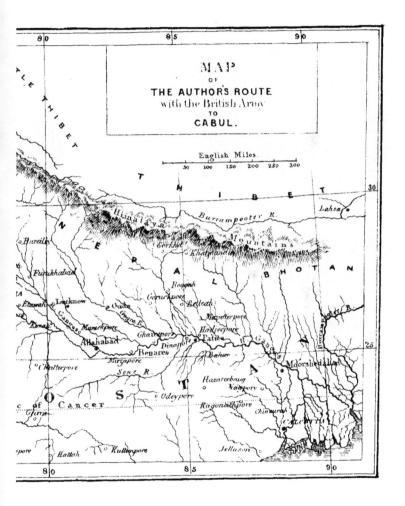